LIVING
TOGETHER

LIVING TOGETHER

COMMUNICATION IN THE UNMARRIED RELATIONSHIP

JOSEPH SIMONS

NELSON-HALL nh CHICAGO

Library of Congress Cataloging in Publication Data
Simons, Joseph
    Living together.

    Includes index.
    1. Unmarried couples. 2. Interpersonal communica-
tion. I. Title.
HQ734.S6   301.11   78-972
ISBN 0-88229-274-9 (cloth)
ISBN 0-88229-599-3 (paper)

Manufactured in the United States of America.

10   9   8   7   6   5   4   3   2   1

Contents

Let's Live Together I

Research for this book just happened. It happened in classrooms when young people began to discuss living together. It happened in therapy sessions when couples explained their decision to remain unmarried. It happened in spontaneous moments when friends talked about their life together. My interest must have been obvious because literally hundreds of people talked with me about life with someone before marriage.

After I had listened to people for about five years, an idea began to form. I decided to write a book about living together. I was uncertain what form the book might take. It was difficult to know for whom the book should be written. In fact, I was faced with more questions than answers. Only one thing was certain: I wanted to share with others the joys and sorrows, the pleasures and pains, the fears and doubts that had been shared with me.

My first impulse, once I had decided to write

1

this book, was to begin interviewing people with experience living together. I had no trouble finding couples willing, even anxious, to talk about their experience. I set up interviews so there would be plenty of time for each person to express thoroughly all opinions and attitudes. Yet, no matter how long an interview lasted, there was always something missing. Compared to my classroom discussions and therapy sessions, the interviews seemed superficial. Still, it was difficult to know exactly what was missing.

My confusion cleared somewhat the day I interviewed Cher, a young woman who had been in one of my classes. She was talking about living with Doug as if it were a smooth and even experience. I knew that was not true. Finally, I was unable to contain myself. I said, "Cher, this isn't the same story you told in class last semester."

"I don't know what you mean."

"You're not mentioning a lot of the reasons you feel the way you do."

"I know."

"Well, why don't you tell your story the way you did last semester?"

"I'm not sure. I guess it's too personal."

"Too personal! It wasn't too personal for an entire classroom filled with students."

"Well, I felt very close to those students. We had shared so much. I felt I had to tell them about the personal side of me."

"I was in that classroom. I heard all about what happened to you and Doug. Why won't you talk about it now?"

"I don't know. It just isn't the same. I don't feel the same as I did then."

"You don't feel the same?"

"Right. The day I talked about the problems Doug and I were having was a special day. The class had been together for about two months. So many people had shared themselves. I felt I knew them. I felt I could trust them. I said things then that I haven't said to anyone else. And that includes Doug."

"So it was a special kind of trust you experienced."

"That's right. I don't know why the day was so special. It just was. I felt trust in a way I never experienced it before. Today I don't feel that way. I can't just turn trust on. Either I feel it or I don't."

As Cher and I continued to talk, I began to realize what she was saying. An atmosphere of trust is not something that occurs easily. It normally builds only over a period of time. No one can schedule trust. Even perfectly planned interviews will not necessarily include it.

When trust does build, however, people are more willing to talk personally about themselves. Toward the end of a class semester, for example, students are often saying things about their life with a partner they had never risked saying before to anyone. I realized that my fascination with the unmarried relationship had developed around such personal statements. By contrast, most of my interviews did not seriously interest me.

A personal world had stimulated me. Intimate thoughts and feelings left me reflecting and wondering. I was not interested in the facts and statistics of the unmarried relationship. I was not concerned about what percentage of the people I talked with had been together two years or more. How often couples living together have sex seemed hardly worth asking. I did not want to spend time finding out how many couples live together against their parents' wishes. My book, if I was to write one, had to deal more intimately with the people I wrote about.

Once More with Feeling

It was easy to say I was interested in the personal side of people. I had no trouble identifying the trust necessary to encourage people to reveal their personal side. The more difficult task was trying to determine just what makes some statements personal and others not. All I knew for certain was that personal discussions, for me, centered on the emotions. I realized I am most interested in the conversations in which people talk intimately of their fears, doubts, joys, and sorrows.

In the *interviews* I conducted, by contrast, people rarely talked about their emotions. Even though they were discussing the most important relationship in their life, few of those interviewed did more than refer to the emotions of love, jealousy, and hate. When such words were mentioned, they were discussed abstractly and analytically.

Most interviews reminded me of early therapy sessions. During the first sessions of therapy, people are apt to talk about their emotions in an abstract way. They seem to want to put distance between themselves and their depression, their anger, and their loneliness. It is as if they expect to solve their emotional conflicts the way they might solve a mathematical puzzle. Some have even said to me, "I came here to get some answers. You've read all those books. Why don't you solve my problems?"

By hiding her emotions, Gail hid from everyone, including herself. Even in group therapy she was not able to express herself. Her description of her relationship with Derek, for example, was too good to be true. She insisted they had a perfect relationship. The rest of the group did not accept this ideal picture, but they were unable to get past Gail's defenses.

Only after months of defensiveness did Gail experience enough trust to tell us about her real feelings. She finally revealed her fears and doubts about her relationship with Derek. Once she began talking, she did not stop for nearly an hour. After she finished I said, "Gail, I have a question."

"Sure. What is it?"

"Why did you tell us that story about you and Derek having the perfect relationship?"

"I had to. Don't you see? If I told you the truth, our relationship might have become as bad as I feared it was."

"You mean by saying your relationship was bad, it might have become that way?"

"Something like that. All I know for sure is I was too terrified to let people see what things were really like."

"But the truth is you and Derek were not relating well at all."

"That's right. Derek and I have been in conflict from the day we moved in together. I didn't want to lie to all of you. I was just terrified of the truth. If I ever said Derek and I were in trouble it just might have come true."

Even if Gail had told us about her troubles from the beginning, she might still have hidden her most important truth. The facts of her unhappy relationship were a minor part of her story. The important truth about Gail was the fear boiling just beneath her story. To try to understand the relationship Gail and Derek had with each other, you had to know about Gail's fear. That fear was central to her life. Everything else about Gail only made sense in relation to her fear.

The real truth of relationships, married or unmarried, straight or gay, close or distant, lies in the world of emotion. All the facts in the world will not make sense unless they are tied to their emotional foundation. To know whether or not couples stay together or separate is not nearly as important as knowing the emotions that keep them together or drive them apart. The emotional truth beneath the unmarried relationship is vital to understanding that relationship.

This book will focus on the emotions that underscore the unmarried relationship. The conclusions drawn in the following chapters are the result of listening to people for long periods of time. None of the material is based on first impressions. The conclusions are extracted from the statements of those I have known intimately. The examples are drawn from interactions with people who have discovered trust slowly. I hope the emotional truth so many have shared with me will help others find their truth. For I am convinced that only by understanding our emotions can we discover intimacy.

What Are You Hiding?

By centering our attention on the emotions, we have given some direction to this book. At the same time, that focus creates problems. For example, there are few similarities between people at the emotional level. The same is true of unmarried relationships. Our fear of expressing feelings is one of the few emotional similarities we all share. Such unexpressed emotion usually causes the problems troubling a couple living together. A young woman may find it impossible to let her partner know how jealous she is of his relationships with other women. A young man might be unable to tell his partner when he fears losing his job. Both might be unwilling to talk about their fears concerning their future. In each case the problems that unexpressed emotion can cause will become more complex with time. Also, there is little hope the resulting difficulties will be relieved until the underlying emotion is expressed.

We are strange creatures. We live in a world of emotion. On any given day we can experience large and small bursts of fear, joy, doubt, frustration, and sorrow. Our inner emotions are a vital part of us. Yet we pass through life and only rarely mention the ebb and flow of emotion to other people. Even those closest to us are often strangers to our inside world. This resistance to expressing feelings is a key problem for those living together. Such couples often create conflict by hiding their emotions from one another.

One student wanted to tell me about his conflict with unexpressed emotion. Yet he was too embarrassed to express it directly. So he wrote a paper and handed it to me one day after class. He said, "I hope this will explain my strange moods over the last few months."

Very early in the paper he talked about moving in with Jill. He said, "*I never have been very good at expressing myself. With Jill somehow it's harder. That's strange. You would think talking to someone close would be easy. But it never was with me. In some ways Jill is the hardest person in the world for me to express my feelings to. And things got worse once we moved in together. From the first night we spent together until now a fear grips me every time I try to tell Jill I love her, or I'm angry with her, or anything else that's personal.*"

Later on in the paper he wrote, "*I know my silence is hard on Jill. She is very insecure and needs a lot of reassurance. I could tell her how much I love her all day and all night and it would not be enough. You can imagine how hard it is on her when she doesn't hear all those things. There were times when I could see the strain was beginning to affect our relationship. I tried to say something personal just to ease the tension. But I couldn't do it. Under the strain, my fear became even greater. Sometimes I felt paralyzed.*"

Toward the end of the paper he said, "*Finally, the lack of expression got to Jill. She sat down with me and said, 'I can't stand it. Either we start communicating with each other or I'm going to have to split.' I knew she meant it. I don't see how she took it as long as she did. I couldn't have taken it myself. So I made all kinds of resolutions. I promised I would begin tomorrow. Always tomorrow. The most I ever got out was a weak, 'I love you.' I knew the end was coming. And I knew a few words from me could turn things around. But I couldn't do anything. I couldn't do anything.*"

The last words of the paper were, "*Jill left me last Friday. I don't know what I'll do.*"

Like a lot of us, this student found it impossible to express certain emotions. Even when he knew his relationship with Jill was threatened he was unable to express his feeling. In fact, his paper would lead us to believe his difficulties increased as the threat increased. There is little reasoning that can be applied to our failure to express emotion. It is one of the great ironies of life. Just when we most want to tell someone about our joy, our sorrow, our happiness, or our loneliness, we freeze in fear.

Our inclination to repress feelings is common enough to be another theme for this book. Very little time will be spent analyzing the reasons behind this tendency. Rather we will look at the tendency itself. We will examine the humanness of the feelings we repress. We will see that almost everyone endures this inclination. We will discuss how others have suffered over, have coped with, and have conquered the fear of exposing an embarrassing inner feeling.

Say It

Most of us repress our feelings. That is a fact. How we react to that fact is another matter altogether. Some people try to find excuses for their lack of emotional expression. Others look into their past life to find reasons to explain why they repress feelings. Still others sit and worry about their inability to say what they feel. All such approaches to repressed emotion accomplish little.

So what should we do with repressed emotion? This book is going to emphasize the value of expressing emotion. This is, of course, easier said than done. Yet the advice is important. The expression of feeling is especially important in the unmarried relationship. I would even chance generalizing by saying, "Couples are happiest when they risk expressing their feelings to one another."

Naturally, I have many reservations about that bit of advice. There is such a thing as a wrong time and place for emotional expression. Expressing a feeling, anger for example, might lead to results couples fear. Letting a partner know about hidden hostility could cause a separation. There are a lot of other qualifications I might place on my too-simple advice. That does not change the truth of the statement: "Couples are happiest when they risk expressing their feelings to one another."

Frank was a young fellow who was afraid to express his anger to his partner, Anne. He knew Anne quite well even before they moved in together. As Frank put it, "Anne has always been afraid of anger. It began in her childhood. When her father would come home drunk and angry, Anne would be absolutely terrified." Consequently, Frank felt compelled to repress his own anger around Anne.

One day Frank came running up to me and said, "You'll never guess what happened."

"What was that?"

"I got really mad at Anne last night. I had been upset for weeks. Some little thing was bothering me, but I couldn't seem to forget it. Finally everything just poured out. I really blew my stack."

"How did Anne react?"

"She was great. That's the beauty of it. Oh, I really upset her. There's no doubt about it. But she didn't fall apart. She even shouted back at me."

"Great."

"Yeah, but that's not the best part. After the fight was over, Anne and I talked. I told her about how afraid I had been to get mad because of her father and all. Then I talked about a lot of other things that have been bothering me."

"That must have been quite a relief."

"You bet it was. Besides, Anne said she could tell when I was upset, because I'd start to sulk. I guess that really bothered her."

"I thought she didn't want to be around anger."

"Oh, that's still there. She said it will take her a long time to get over it. She was really nervous while we were fighting. But she also told me she would rather face this anger thing and get past it."

"It sounds like talking things out was the best thing for both of you."

"You bet it was. I feel just great."

Not every expression of feeling turns out this well. Frank's angry outburst might have led to a separation. Anne might have gone into her shell instead of accepting his anger. A lot of problems could have developed. But they didn't. The truth is that the dire consequences we fear from such emotional encounters seldom occur.

Two people living together risk much more by not expressing feelings than they ever do by expressing them. The greatest single obstacle to harmony between couples living together is repressed feelings. The unexpressed anger, jealousy, and fear bring doubt and suspicion to most relationships. One unexpressed feeling leads to another. A person who leaves feelings unexpressed urges a partner to do the same. Then it is all to easy to fall into a pattern of leaving emotions hidden. At such a point they have already started to become indifferent.

Let's Live Together

This book is going to center on the living-together relationship. The emphasis will be directed at the emotions underlying that relationship. We will look at jealousy, anger, and fear. Our consideration of communication and independence will also be in the context of emotion and its impact on relationships.

This book will strongly urge couples living together to express their feelings to each other. My own experience in talking and working with others has convinced me that most relationship problems stem from the inability or the unwillingness to express emotion. This bit of advice will not be stated as a rule. There is no such thing as a rule when it comes to dealing with interpersonal relationships. It is to be hoped, however, that as the book progresses, couples will see the value of expressing their emotions to one another.

I'm Scared 2

Fear is a part of all love relationships. Those who have been close to someone know about both the logical and the irrational fears that emerge in serious relationships. It seems logical, for example, to worry about a partner's sickness; we can all accept this kind of worry as normal and healthy. We can even admit such fears to others. The irony of our attitude is that the logical fears we are willing to accept are not the ones that most trouble us.

Possibly because we are not so free to accept them, irrational fears bother us more than logical ones. It is precisely when our fears seem unfounded that we grow seriously upset. Our jealousy, for example, is greatest when it appears groundless. We often know there is no sexual or emotional pull between a partner and the person we fear. Yet the fear will not disappear. At that point, the sheer irrationality of our fear only intensifies its impact.

Fear, when it is not founded in the reality we

can understand, is embarrassing. We have somehow identified irrational fear with weakness and
foolishness. Consequently, we are afraid to mention to anyone, even our partner, the unreasonable fears that grip us from time to time. For
many of us, saying we are fearful is like saying
we are weak and unstable. We would rather not
say to anyone, "I'm being weak and foolish
today." It seems so much better to hide our fear
and try to deal with it ourselves.

Irrational fears had Susan nearly frantic the
day she came to see me. A lot of things frightened
her, but she was most upset by her fear that Rick
would leave her.

"There is just no reason for me to be afraid,"
she told me with a great deal of anxiety.

"Why do you say that?"

"Well, it's crazy. Rick hardly knows any
other women and yet I'm afraid he will fall in
love with someone else."

"I'm not sure I understand."

"I don't understand, either. All I can say is I
have this terrible fear Rick is going to leave me
for some other woman."

"But you said he hardly knows any other
women."

"That's right. Now tell me that's not crazy.
Every time he looks at a woman or a woman
looks at him, chills run through me. Even if the
woman is just selling him a magazine I can get
jealous."

"Have you talked with Rick about this?"

"Oh, sure. He just says I'm being stupid. And
he's right. I am being stupid."

"There's a lot more to it than that."

"Like what?"

"Well, just because your fears are illogical doesn't mean they're not real."

"That's for sure."

"Those fears are having a real impact on your relationship. It would be a mistake to try to ignore them."

"I guess so. I don't know."

"What do you mean, you don't know?"

"I don't know how seriously I can take my fears. You've got to admit they're pretty stupid."

Susan never did look seriously at her fear. She could not get past her own decision that her fear was "stupid." Rick only reinforced her attitudes. He knew he was not attracted to anyone else so he continued to dismiss Susan's fear. Neither of them was able to look past the immediate logic of the situation. If Susan had been seriously ill, then it would have been reasonable for her to be worried. Rick himself would probably have been upset. More important, he would have accepted Susan's need to worry over her health. As long as her fear was not logical, however, neither Susan nor Rick could look at it seriously.

When we concentrate our attention on the logic of a fear, we cannot see that fear clearly. In reality, there is much about fear that is not logical. Probably fear is, in the final analysis, more irrational than logical. Consequently, we must look beyond reason to understand the importance of fear. In the case of Susan and Rick, for example, the importance of the irrational fear lay in the impact it was having on their relationship. If nothing else, their life together was being affected by Susan's fear. That would seem reason enough for them to take the fear seriously.

Listen, I'm Serious

The question is: How do we go about taking irrational fears seriously? To understand the answer, we will first look at the way we instinctively treat fear. Most of us think we are taking fear seriously when we listen carefully to fearful people and try to explain to them how unreasonable their fear is. Reactions like, "You don't have anything to worry about," and "Don't be silly," and "You have yourself worked up over nothing," are common enough to be stereotyped. It is as if we know only one way to respond to an irrational fear.

To understand the impact of such reactions, we need only turn the situation around. We can project ourselves back to a time when we personally faced an irrational fear and heard someone say, "Quit worrying about it, will you?" Attitudes like that increased our frustration, our anxiety, and even our fear. We already knew our fear was irrational. No one needed to tell us about that. By being told about the unreasonableness of our fear, we became more embarrassed by our reaction. That embarrassment then planted the fear deeper and made it more difficult to cope with.

So how do we take irrational fears seriously? By treating them, first of all, as fears, and only secondly as irrational. The most important thing about a fear is not its rationale. The significant thing is the inner emotional turmoil it causes. We treat another person's fears seriously by remembering how painful it is to cope with fear and its embarrassment. Reminding a person how irrational a fear is only increases that fear. The most helpful thing we can do for fearful people is to let them be fearful and accept them in spite of their turmoil.

During a trip to this area, Dave, a relative of mine, told me about his wife's fear of social events. He said, "It's really gotten pretty bad. We hardly go anywhere anymore. Carol actually gets nauseated in most social situations. I've tried to explain to her that she has nothing to worry about. She is, after all, well liked by everyone. The trouble is, even when I say something reassuring like that, she gets upset. I honestly don't know what to do."

We talked for a long time—most of the night. Dave finally began to see that Carol's reaction was pretty human. More than anything else I think he saw the value of listening to Carol's fear. He normally cut her off as soon as she deviated from the logical. He decided he should try listening carefully to everything Carol said about herself and her fear. Carol's fear was a very important part of her. Unless Dave spent time trying to learn about that fear, he would never understand a significant part of Carol.

A letter soon after our talk contained good news. Dave wrote, *"Things have changed. I'm not sure how or why, but they really have changed. I am beginning to understand Carol's fear. I was so disgusted by her irrationality that I never realized the trauma she was experiencing. It has been painful for her. Now that I am more sensitive to her fear I wonder how she endured my adding to the turmoil she was in for so long."*

Later on in the letter, Dave said, *"You should see the change in Carol. She still has her fear of social situations, but it's much milder now. She doesn't stay up half the night worrying about what she might have done or said wrong. Now she goes right off to sleep. The other night she even suggested it might be fun to have Frank and Gail over for dinner. I could hardly believe my ears.*"

There are people who automatically suggest that listening is the answer to problems like the one Dave and Carol faced. As Carol's father said to me, "If Dave would just listen to Carol, everything would be all right. He wouldn't even have to say anything." There is some truth in that statement. People so seldom listen to us that the experience is often therapeutic in itself. I am sure Carol would have felt much better if Dave had taken time just to listen to her.

The problem with that bit of advice is the subtle attitude it conveys. Those who say that "just listening" is going to be the answer also suggest that those in turmoil are a bit foolish. The entire attitude that "you don't even have to say anything" implies there is little to be understood. Finally, another troubling attitude is sometimes implicit in the "just listen" advice: it suggests that the listener is in a position superior to the person suffering the fear.

Dave finally understood Carol because he listened to her emotions as well as her words. When Dave listened to Carol's words only, he was out of contact with her. Her words, isolated from her emotions, were unreal. They made no sense. By contrast, they took on meaning only within the context of her fear.

Dave reached Carol by doing more than "just listening." He reached beyond her words and made contact with her fear. He could assume no superior attitude. He knew what fear was. He finally understood Carol at the emotional level. When he was willing to admit to himself he could be just as upset, he was able to touch Carol and be a comfort to her.

Poor Me

We bring a lot of fear to the unmarried relationship. One of the greatest is the fear we are unlovable. Most of us are frightened that, underneath it all, we have very little of value. So we enjoy being with someone who thinks we are special. Somehow our fear is relieved even by the presence of a person who likes us. Consequently, it is not surprising that most people who begin to live together do so primarily to be with a person who cares for them.

Our fear of being unlovable is so fundamental that it can affect everything in life. Some people are so certain they are inadequate that fear follows them everywhere. They fear meeting people, fear being alone, fear speaking before people, fear being in closed places—and even fear noises in the night. Some psychologists think the fear of being unlovable is so basic that it is at the root of every other fear. That may be only a theory, but it has the ring of truth.

The act of living together strikes at the root of the fear of inadequacy. By moving in with someone who truly cares about us we are challenging our inadequate feelings. We put ourselves in a position to be loved. Paradoxically, the unmarried relationship also makes it possible for the person who cares to hurt us. Separation is a daily possibility. It is not surprising, under such circumstances, for couples to face serious fears. In fact, it might be more accurate to say unmarried couples rarely escape fear in their attempts to relate.

Jane gave me some insight into the fears implicit in living together. She had been with Bob for only about a week when she started having nightmares. At first, she paid little attention to them. Then, when they continued, she came to see me.

"I've never had nighmares in my whole life. Why should they begin now when I'm so happy?"

"Isn't there anything you are afraid of?"

"No, not that I can think of."

"Come on, now. Living together isn't all that easy."

"What do you mean?"

"Moving in with someone is an important change in anyone's life. Surely you don't make a big change like that without being frightened."

"You're right. I try not to admit it, but I am afraid."

"What are you afraid of?"

"I'm scared Bob will leave me. I know that's crazy, but it's there. I guess things have been too good."

"Too good?"

"Yeah. I can't understand why a great guy like Bob would want to move in with me."

"Why wouldn't he want to move in with you?"

"If you really knew me you wouldn't ask me that question."

"The real you isn't very lovable."

"I know it sounds corny, but it's true."

"I don't think it sounds corny at all. I think it sounds very human. Most people I know are afraid that underneath it all they aren't very lovable."

"Is that the reason for my nightmares? Do you think I'm scared Bob will see my ugly side?"

"It's certainly possible."

A great irony surrounds our fear of being unlovable. If *we* were going to make the world the way it "ought" to be, we would probably create people who really liked themselves. Our adequate people would then be free to reach out to others with care and concern. That world of love would be a great place to live.

The real world is backwards from our ideal world. We struggle with a terrible fear that, underneath the face we show to the world, we are a person no one could love. With such an attitude toward ourselves, we constantly fear we will be discovered. Our preoccupation with ourselves then makes it difficult to turn outward in love toward others.

Two people who begin living together are often trying to turn the real world around. They hope that with one other person they can enter a state where two people will find one another lovable. Then they might be able to turn away from their preoccupation with inadequacy. The step is tentative and frightening. A wrong move could end the relationship overnight. No wonder fear enters into the world of bliss. Fear and love are not incompatible. They regularly exist side by side.

Let Me Show You Something

Those who enter the unmarried relationship must be prepared to deal with irrational fear. For only by taking such fear seriously can we hope to have a healthy relationship.

Listening to a lover's fear is not an act of charity. If we listen only because we hope to help, we lose our chance to share an intimate revelation. The partner courageous enough to reveal personal fear is the charitable one. That partner is saying to us, "I trust you enough to show you the secret and vulnerable part of myself." We are given permission to look into a most fascinating part of the world—the inner world of another person.

If our first step into our partner's world is sensitive and understanding, we might be allowed to go further. That special person just might invite us back to see other thoughts, feelings, and emotions. There is no greater gift. Our initial look into the world of a love is especially important. And expressed fear is often the first attempt by a partner to say, "I love you enough to show you a part of myself I've never shown to anyone."

I had one young woman in therapy who had a particularly difficult time expressing her fears. She was helped greatly by Bill, the fellow she was living with. He responded to her fears with a lot of patience and understanding. Then, at a time when things appeared to going smoothly, Karen got a big shock.

"Last night Bill really surprised me," Karen said with a look of bewilderment.

"Surprised you? How was that?"

"Well, I was telling him how frightened I was in the night. I had to get up about three in the morning to see if someone was in our apartment. Anyway, Bill just burst into tears."

"Burst into tears? What do you mean?"

"Just that. Bill started crying. He told me how fearful he was that something was mentally wrong with me. He said every time that I get frightened, he gets frightened too."

"How did you react?"

"At first I told him he didn't need to worry. I tried to explain to him that my fears weren't all that real. Then the irony of the situation got me."

"The irony of the situation?"

"Yeah. Here I was telling Bill not to worry. That's the very thing I don't want him to do to me."

"So what did you do?"

"I listened. I even asked some questions. I really tried to hear Bill's fears and understand them."

"It's not easy, is it?"

"Oh, boy! It sure isn't. I kept wanting to jump in with advice."

"Were you able to resist?"

"Pretty well. The important thing was what happened to me. I really got a look at Bill. I've been so busy telling Bill about me that I never saw his emotional side. I had no idea Bill knew what fear was."

Karen's self-revelations encouraged Bill to attempt the same thing. It took him a long time to reveal his sensitive side. He could finally tell her about all the fears and doubts he was having. It was as if he were returning the gift of openness to Karen. She nearly missed the point. She almost shut him off by telling him his fears were groundless. Luckily, she realized in time that the irrationality of his fears was not important. The important thing was Bill's desire to show his emotional self.

The Courage to Be Scared

The inner world of emotion is confusing.

True emotional reactions are often different from our expectations. For example, we commonly think we are being courageous when we hide our fear from others. The truth is, if we think about it for a while, we are embarrassed by our fear. When we conceal our fear we are most often afraid we will be seen as weak and inadequate. Far from being a courageous act, hiding our fear is commonly an act of timidity.

The courageous person is the one who can say, "Yes, I get frightened at times. Sometimes I get scared to death. I often hide my fear from you. But that's not what I want. I want you to know about my fear because I want you to know about me." That sort of admission is particularly difficult in a living-together situation. The admission of fear leaves us vulnerable to the very person we would like to impress. It takes a great deal of courage to admit, "Even though I'm not the person I would like to be, I want you to know who I am."

One student I knew found it extremely difficult to tell Nancy, the woman he was living with, about his fear she would leave him. He told me that if she really wanted to leave him he would rather not influence her decision. He thought if Nancy knew about his fear she would stay with him out of some misguided compassion. So Jerry continued to hide his fear until one night it just overwhelmed him. As he told me afterward, "I just couldn't stand it any longer. I broke down and told Nancy how frightened I was she might leave me."

"How do you feel now?"

"Still a little embarrassed. But mostly good."

"Mostly good?"

"Yes. I finally feel personally involved with

Nancy. Before last night I liked her, but I never really felt close. Somehow by letting her see my most embarrassing emotions I was drawn closer to her."

"And you don't think you influenced her decision to stay with you?"

"You know, that isn't important any longer. Even if I did influence her to stay with me, that's all right. I know I want us to stick together. So why shouldn't she know that, too?"

"Your attitudes have really changed."

"You bet they have. All because I gave Nancy a peek at my fear. It's hard to believe how much I resisted letting her see me frightened. I was fighting the very thing that finally drew us close."

"That was a brave thing you did."

"Brave? I don't know about that. I know it was hard, but it was sure worth it. I've never felt so close to Nancy."

Jerry was hesitant to admit it, but he was courageous to let Nancy know about his fear that she would leave him. He had all sorts of logical reasons for avoiding that admission. Yet it was his exposure to Nancy that finally drew him close to her. All the signs of affection, the shared intimacies, and the desires to be close did not achieve what that one fearful revelation accomplished. In a moment, Jerry moved from distance to intimacy.

A moment of revelation will not bring permanent intimacy. The feeling of closeness will pass in time. Then another revelation of inner feeling will be necessary to sustain closeness. There is no such thing as achieving a goal in interpersonal relations. We must rather practice an art. Each revealed feeling clears the way for more feelings to emerge. There is no end to the process.

Living together is best when it is sustained by the revelation of feelings. To share the fears, doubts, joys, and sorrows of life with someone who cares is what living together can mean. It often begins after we have the courage to reveal that first embarrassing fear. That fear gives our partner a glimpse of our inner world. The step can be the beginning of a journey—a journey into the world of love.

$Take$ $a$$Chance$ 3

If I were forced to sum up this book in one word, that word would be risk. Risk is at the heart of every good living-together relationship. Such relationships flourish because partners are willing to risk sharing with one another the intimate feelings, the embarrassing feelings, the awkward feelings they would rather keep to themselves.

Couples unable to take risks will let feelings build. Even the minor irritations inevitable in such close circumstances will go unexpressed. Lovers can so easily put off telling one another about little habits that annoy. One repressed feeling leads to another, and before long minor grievances can become massive. Meanwhile the habit of not expressing feelings is growing and dominating the relationship.

When small annoyances go unexpressed regularly, serious conflicts follow. By the time such conflits develop, the habit of nonexpression has become a pattern. The partners have built a wall around their feelings. They will not let one another penetrate that wall and look at personal emotion.

Whoever said, "Love is hard work," must have been talking about risk. There is no easy way to express feelings. The fears and doubts that accompany any expression of feeling are inescapable. If two people want to turn their affection into a love relationship, they must be willing to risk. No matter how close we might be to someone, no matter how secure we feel in a relationship, no matter how much we trust another, there will always be feelings we would rather not express.

Whenever I think of risk, I think of Sherry and Ron. Their relationship appeared to be so good. They were obviously crazy about each other from the beginning. When Sherry told me their life together was a shambles, I was shocked.

"It looks like Ron and I are going to have to split," Sherry told me, nearly choking on the words.

"Split! I thought you guys were happy."

"We were. In fact, I never knew living with someone could be so good. We enjoyed each other when we were together, and missed each other when we had to be separated."

"You'll have to give me a second to pull myself together, Sherry. I just assumed you and Ron would never separate."

"So did I."

"Well, what happened?"

"I'm not sure. I only know that after we moved in together things began to change."

"Change? In what way?"

"Ron stopped talking about his feelings. He refused to tell me when he was down or depressed. Instead, he would close up inside and sulk."

"Did you ask him about it?"

"Not really."

"So you stopped expressing your feelings, too."

"I just figured Ron must have enough on his mind. I didn't want to put any more pressure on him."

"You just stopped communicating."

"Yes, but it wasn't that bad. We still had fun together. We both like sports and camping and things like that. When we were active we still enjoyed each other."

"But your relationship kept deteriorating."

"Yes. The little things that irritated me soon became serious. Before long I stopped sharing my life with Ron. He became like a stranger to me."

"Then what happened?"

"I started to hate Ron. All those little irritations grew and got out of hand. I hated him for not talking to me, for letting our life together go to pieces, for making me suffer. Almost everything he did made me hate Ron more."

"But you still couldn't tell Ron you hated him."

"Oh, no! Now it's too late. I don't even want to tell Ron I'm splitting. I would rather just leave him a note."

Ron and Sherry may represent an extreme. Most couples will at least make some attempt to express their feelings. However, I have talked with many who never do achieve any honest attempt.

Why?

Any discussion of risk will eventually evoke the question, "Why?" A countless number of people have asked me, "Why is it so difficult for me to express my most important feelings?" Any number of reasons could be cited. Some say childhood experiences account for their difficulty in expressing themselves. Others think they were born with the fears that prevent them from revealing their emotions. Still others blame society for their failure.

There may never be a final answer to the question, "Why am I afraid to express my feelings?" The debate might go on endlessly. Even if we did find an answer, however, it would not bring an end to our fear. The fear of expressing feelings is a fact of life. The most important question, in view of that fact, is not, "Why am I afraid?" but rather, "How am I going to cope with my fear?"

Ironically, the only way to deal with the fear that surrounds personal feelings is to risk expressing them. When we express a feeling in spite of our fear, we discover the fear will not destroy us. The terrible doubts that might undermine our need to express anger, for example, will grow even as we look for the cause of our anger. By contrast, those who express anger as soon as they feel it will experience only a minimum amount of fear.

The risk of expressing feelings is particularly important for those who live together. A legal bond helps hold married couples together when they are under pressure. Partners living together have no such outside force to cling to. Consequently, it is crucial for them to face the strains on their relationship immediately. There is no time to wonder what causes the fear of expressing their feelings.

Of all the students who have asked me about this fear, one stands out more clearly than the others. I remember Barbara primarily because she was so determined to know the reason why she hid her feelings. In fact, her preoccupation with the question made her blind to almost everything else.

"I get absolutely petrified whenever I try to tell Alan how I feel," Barbara said to me one day.

"That happens to a lot of people."

"But Alan and I have been living together for four years. We share the same bed. Surely it isn't normal for me to be so upset every time I want to express myself."

"I don't know what you mean by 'normal.' I do know that most people experience fear when they are trying to express personal feelings."

"Not with someone who is so close."

"Yes! Many couples—married and unmarried—find it nearly impossible to share personal emotion."

"Why? It doesn't make any sense. Why should I be so afraid? Is it because I'm afraid people might reject me?"

"I'm really not sure why people find it so difficult."

"I always thought I was homely. Maybe that's why I repress my feelings."

"Maybe. I couldn't say. The fact is that you are afraid, and the important question is, 'What are you going to do about it?'"

"Yeah, I know. But there has to be a reason. I keep thinking if I could just figure out why I'm so tense about it, things might go better between Alan and me."

"It's perfectly normal to wonder why you can't express your feelings. I keep wondering the same thing. But I can assure you all the thinking in the world won't help you reveal them."

"There has to be some reason for all that fear."

"You aren't hearing what I'm saying. I admit there may be a reason. I just want you to understand that finding the reason will not solve your problem. You will still have to learn how to deal with your fear."

"I know. But I still can't help feeling that if I could just figure out why I'm afraid, Alan and I could smooth things out."

I continued to talk with Barbara for over an hour. She never did grasp what I was trying to tell her. She was blinded by her desire to discover the reason behind her fear. What she failed to understand was how her preoccupation was allowing her fear to build. Each minute she spent looking for her answer was one more minute for her fear to grow.

I'm So Lonely

It would be perfectly normal at this point to wonder why we should bother expressing our feelings at all. The fears we must face if we are open to others are reason enough to want to avoid any expression of feeling. At times, it seems almost unnatural to tell others about the embarrassing feelings of sadness, doubt, and loneliness that bother us so often.

The most significant reason for revealing ourselves lies inside of us. Unless others can see the emotions that make us unique, we will remain strangers to them. It is our emotional center that gives us our uniqueness as a person. We are different from others to the extent that we are shy or outgoing, sensitive or warm. A combination of these emotional traits makes us unique. To the extent that we hide these attitudes we also hide an important part of ourselves.

When we cover our feelings we can be lonely in the midst of a crowd. When we engage in nothing but talk about topics of general interest, we remain just another person. People learn about our ideas but they do not learn about us. They never learn what upsets us, what pleases us, what stimulates us, what causes us pain. But the loneliness that comes from remaining hidden grows slowly. We can sustain a faceless existence for a long time. Sooner or later, however, loneliness will emerge and cause us grief.

Loneliness is always painful. When it becomes part of a couple's relationship, the pain is acute. People living together who fail to reveal inner feelings to one another will eventually find themselves lonely in each other's presence. There may be no greater suffering.

In Marlene's case, it was painful just to listen to her talk about her relationship with Lars. She was close to tears when she told me, "We have been together for one year, and I don't think I can stand it any longer."

"What's wrong?"

"That's part of the problem. I don't know for sure what's wrong."

"What do you mean?"

"Well, take last Tuesday. That was our first anniversary together. I spent all day preparing a terrific dinner. I spent a lot of money for steak and wine, I even bought some flowers for the table. I was hoping against hope for a great evening."

"And Lars didn't even notice."

"Oh, he noticed, all right. He thanked me and gave me a big kiss. He even made a special toast. No, Lars was trying just as hard as I was."

"Well, what was the problem?"

"The problem began after we ran out of small talk. We reminisced about our first meeting, laughed over some of our funny experiences together, and chatted about the future. But after about thirty minutes there was nothing left to say. We ran out of talk."

"You ran out of talk?"

"Yes! That's when the trouble begins. As soon as our conversation stops, a terrible silence grows up between us. Every time I try to break the silence, I feel like I just create more strain. Before that particular night was over, I wanted to scream. Never in my life have I felt so lonely, so isolated, and so unloved."

Marlene and I continued to talk most of the night. It turned out that she and Lars represented a classic example of unexpressed feelings.

They lived together, liked each other, and wished the best for one another. But for various reasons they chose to keep their inner worlds hidden. They had great fun together when they were occupied with things outside themselves. As long as they were going to a movie, playing games together, or engaged in some other vigorous activity, they were happy.

Their problems started when "there was

nothing left to say." They could spend only so long talking about the day's activities, the movie they had just seen, or their plans for the future. If they were to talk further, they would have had to risk exposing their inner worlds of fear, frustration, or joy. Neither could take the chance and so they let their conversation die. At that point, they could only experience their distance from one another. Loneliness was inevitable.

Let Me Touch You

In contrast to those who maintain distance because they fear to show their feelings, some find the courage to reveal themselves to one another. They talk about their doubts, misgivings, frustrations, and anger. They even risk showing irritation at a lover. To say to someone you love, "I really got mad at you today," is the ultimate in risk-taking. Such a burst of anger just might end a relationship. The truth is, an outburst is not as likely to end it as to strengthen it. Yet the risk is always there.

Partners who reveal themselves to one another cannot conceive of running out of things to say. Often the process of talking is painful, and they might wish they did not have to share so much pain. But there is never any danger they will wonder what to talk about. And the process is not all pain. Even when a conversation dwells on doubts and misgivings, a great closeness is involved. Partners often say about such serious conversations, "I felt as if I was really being seen for the first time. I revealed some of the ugliest parts of myself, and I was still loved!"

Those who reveal themselves openly to one another do so for reasons that reach past the risk and the pain. They let out their inner secrets so that they can be intimately known by one other person. The loneliness that is part of all of us dissipates when another person begins to understand just what we are like in the inner world we normally keep hidden. Then we see that revealing our feelings is worth every embarrassment, every fear, and every doubt that make the risks seem foolish.

I never knew anyone quite so withdrawn, insecure, and inadequate as Loren. When he was in my class, he rarely said anything. The few times he did talk he could barely be heard. He always managed to hide in some corner of the room so that few of us would notice him. Hiding seemed to be part of Loren's personality.

Two years after that class ended, Loren came to see me. The change in him was spectacular. I hardly recognized him. I remember saying, "My gosh. You have really changed, Loren. You're looking just great."

"You have no idea how much I've changed."

"Tell me about it."

"I couldn't tell you one little part of it in less than three weeks."

"I can imagine. But please give me some idea what happened to you."

"The only short way to express it is to say that Beth happened to me."

"That sounds good."

"Yeah, Beth and I moved in together about the time your class was ending. That was great, but there's a lot more to it than that."

"More to it than what?"

"Well, if I only say we moved in together I

leave out how important it was that it was Beth I moved in with."

"I'm not sure what you're saying."

"When Beth and I moved in together, it was great for a while. I started to gain some confidence in myself and open up a little. But after a few months things got bad again. I was beginning to withdraw and crawl back in my shell."

"Is that when Beth came through for you?"

"She sure did! She just wouldn't let me cover up. She told me how much she cared for me, how painful it was for her to watch me withdraw, how close she felt when I told her about whatever was bothering me. She opened herself completely."

"That's fantastic."

"You have no idea. But I was still too frightened to open up."

"Even with Beth practically begging you?"

"Even with Beth practically begging me. I was just terrified that once Beth saw what I was really like, she would pack up and leave. I needed her too much to take a chance on her leaving."

"But you finally did open up."

"A little at a time I let Beth inside. The more I opened myself, the more she loved me. It just kept baffling me. The more I told Beth about this ugly person I was hiding from her, the closer she came."

"So Beth lured you out of your closed world."

"I don't know how she did it. But yes! Beth lured me out into the open."

"And now?"

"Now I don't hate myself any more. Thanks to Beth I get along pretty well with myself."

The change in Loren was dramatic. He acted

more relaxed. He spoke with confidence. He even looked better. His life of risk with Beth had changed him completely. Beth opened him up to himself. They were now vulnerable to one another. Their risks had drawn them close and made them intimate. In an incredibly short period of time, Beth and Loren had grown from friendly strangers to intimate lovers. Their relationship had taken root the way every living-together relationship must if friends are ever to become lovers.

Take Your Choice

In the final analysis, each of us has a choice. We may choose to risk opening ourselves to our lover, or we may decide to keep our emotions concealed. The choice is not uncomplicated, however. If we choose, for example, to remain closed to others, we will inevitably suffer great loneliness. That loneliness may not be evident during any single decision to conceal our feelings from others. In fact, over a long period of time we may not experience loneliness as a result of hiding our emotional self. Sooner or later, however, trapping our emotions inside will take its toll.

On the other hand, I have met a number of people who make a clear decision to remain closed. For a myriad of reasons, they choose the loneliness they experience. In many of those cases the choice seems reasonable. For them the risk of opening themselves seems too frightening. So they make a conscious decision to be lonely.

I was reminded of the fear risk can create the day I was talking to Anita. She seemed so distant when she said, "I have never revealed my feelings to Harvey, and I never intend to."

"You have been together for a year and have never revealed your feelings," I said, a bit startled.

"That's right! Outside of a few involuntary outbursts, I've kept my feelings inside."

"I don't understand."

"After my marriage, I decided two things. I will never be married again, and I will not let anyone inside."

"What happened in your marriage?"

"I let the guy in and really loved him. I have never been so open in my entire life. I thought he was doing the same thing. I thought we were close."

"And?"

"He didn't even bother to say goodbye. He just left me a note."

"That's terrible."

"You don't know how terrible it was. It was months before I calmed down. I'll never go through that again for anyone."

"Where does that leave you in your relationship with Harvey?"

"We have a pretty good relationship. We do a lot of things together, enjoy each other's company, share expenses, and do all the other things roommates usually do."

"But no revealed feelings."

"No revealed feelings!"

"Don't you get awfully lonely?"

"Of course I do. At times I just want to cry. I want to tell Harvey about all the sad things, the happy things, the fearful things, and the light things I am feeling. I want to tell him because I know he would understand. I need someone to understand. But I would rather endure my loneliness than ever again face the hurt that followed my marriage."

Anita had good reasons for hiding her feelings. A lot of people do. My fear is that many people fail to realize the price they must pay. They do not understand, as Anita did, that a great loneliness follows those who keep their emotions concealed. Those who can stand the pain of being alone are free to keep their feelings to themselves. Those who long to alleviate that loneliness must risk bringing them into the open.

Listen to Me 4

We rarely listen to one another. No research psychologist has to reach this conclusion for us. We need only look around to notice how seldom people listen. There are times when it appears someone is listening. We will see a person pause and look intently while someone else is speaking. That looks like listening. Yet, if we could see inside the listener's head, we would probably see mostly personal reflections. Very little attention would be given to the speaker.

The argument is the clearest example of not listening. Any time we are listening to and detached from an argument, we will observe non-listening in the extreme. One person will drive a point home with emotion and enthusiasm. As soon as that person pauses, another person will make a new point with little regard for what has just been said. More often than not, the argument will be pursued on two completely different planes. The detached listener will often find no point of disagreement. At the same time, those arguing will be in emotional turmoil over their conflict.

Most of us admit we are guilty of non-listening at times. We know what it is to be so consumed by our own thoughts and feelings that we completely miss what is said to us. This can happen to us in an argument and in a casual conversation. We are probably unaware of just how often we lose the sense of what others are trying to communicate. At the same time, few of us would claim to be free of falling into this kind of extreme.

Of all the people I have ever met, Sam had probably perfected nonlistening more than anyone. He was a college classmate who astonished everyone with his ability to talk without a break. He could dominate a conversation indefinitely. Some of my classmates even tested his ability. One fellow stayed with Sam for ten hours. He did everything he could think of to bother Sam. Nothing broke Sam's control of the conversation. Sam was not disturbed by boredom, anger, or disquiet. He could talk through it all.

A relative of mine at a nearby college described a classmate of his who was just as dominant. He told me about Frank who seemed to be Sam's match. We could hardly wait to introduce Sam and Frank so we could observe the results. All of the people who knew Sam and Frank were also anxious to observe the meeting. We carefully planned the day so that Sam would meet Frank early in the morning. We also made certain that Sam and Frank would never be alone. We took turns observing and tape recording the great conversation.

We managed to introduce Sam and Frank before breakfast at about seven o'clock in the morning. That was the beginning of the marathon. At first there was a struggle for dominance. Both men wanted to tell the most impressive story, talk the longest, and control the direction of the conversation. Soon that became futile. Both had too much experience to be dominated. So after about four hours, they began taking turns. One would tell his story and when he had finished the other would tell his story. That went on for hours. The rest of us grew weary and bored. But Sam and Frank seemed to pick up enthusiasm as the day wore on.

Around eleven o'clock that evening Sam and Frank said goodbye. They told one another how much they enjoyed the day. There was little evidence during the sixteen hours they were together that either one had done any listening. More accurately, listening was done only to catch every opportunity to regain control of the conversation. The sixteen hours of the tapes were never played. The original conversation was boring enough. No one was prepared for a replay.

Over the years I have thought of that experience with Frank and Sam. It was the classical example of nonlistening. I have never found anyone quite as dedicated to talking as those two guys. Yet, a lot of people have come close. The main difference between the Sam-Frank syndrome and the rest of us is in the subtle way most of us cover our drive to talk. We would never want others to know how compulsive we really are.

The truth is that most of us have a good bit of Sam and Frank in us. We like to talk and tell others about ourselves. It is difficult for us to stop and listen to someone else. We can be angry at this tendency. We can even confess it to others. But few of us ever take serious steps to overcome our inability to listen.

I Can't Hear You

Over the years I have asked many people why they personally find it difficult to listen to others. Some have said they get bored by other people. Some have admitted they like to talk more than listen. Others fear they will not be noticed unless they make themselves heard. There are still others who find their compulsion to talk quite baffling. As one lady said to me, "After I leave people, I think of a million things I wanted to ask them. Then I get kind of sad thinking that I am so selfish."

One of the most interesting replies to my question about listening came from several people. They said, in one way or another, that they already knew what people were going to say. One young man even prided himself in being able to finish sentences for other people. He considered this skill very important and apparently had worked hard to develop it. He never thought of his skill as a finely developed block to listening.

Maybe we just spend too much time inside our own mind. Because we listen to our own thoughts and feelings so much we think of anything else as irrelevant. After spending our life thinking and feeling in one particular way, it is difficult to try to see the world as another person might.

By the time Kay decided to talk to me, she was about ready to move out on Scott. She was upset because she feared Scott was losing interest in her.

"What makes you think Scott is losing interest in you?" I asked her.

"Well, he rarely expresses any feeling."

"You mean he used to express his feelings more than he does now?"

"No, not really."

"What then?"

"The thing is I expected him to start expressing more feeling as time went on."

"Why did you expect that?"

"I guess because I've always had his undivided attention."

"Are you sure Scott was giving you his undivided attention?"

"Well, he hardly ever says anything."

"You mean his silence made you think he was giving you his undivided attention."

"Yes, I guess that's it."

"Have you ever thought Scott might be naturally quiet?"

"But if he wasn't paying attention to what I was saying, what was he thinking about?"

"Have you ever asked him?"

"No, but—"

"I think it's only fair to ask Scott about his real feelings before you assume he's losing interest in you."

As it turned out, Scott, like many other quiet people, thinks about a lot of things while others are talking. He listens to people about as closely as most of us. The only difference was that Kay assumed he was listening attentively to her. He actually listened to Kay about as carefully as she listened to him. Scott could repeat what Kay said to him on any given occasion. But most of the time that he appeared to be listening his mind was actually drifting elsewhere.

Most of us make assumptions about what others are thinking and feeling. We can assume we know what they are going to say. We can think we know how they look at life. We can even, as Kay did, think we know their attitudes toward us. Such assumptions can be correct. They can also be wrong. In a close relationship, however, our false assumptions are always dangerous.

We will never cease to make judgments based on our own feelings. That is natural. The danger lies in our failure to check those conclusions against reality. What we judge to be listening may be boredom. What we conclude is anger may be an upset stomach. What we think is love may be a pleasant disposition. Our own reaction to someone is only part of the listening process. The other half of listening implies we listen to what others say about themselves.

Don't Disturb Me

There is another, more fundamental, reason why most of us find it difficult to listen to others. In order to really listen, we have to enter their world. We have to try looking at life from their point of view. This is difficult. We are so used to our own attitudes that it is almost impossible to imagine seeing life differently.

The most difficult point of view to adopt involves another person's value system. Most of us find it hard even to accept the fact that others have values different from our own. If we orient our life around making money, for example, it is disturbing to listen to someone who is casual about money. Somehow we find it difficult to say, "Well, he just has a different outlook on life." Rather, we normally find another value-system a personal challenge. Only a few of us can overlook a difference in values and accept others for what they are.

Our natural tendency, when we are confronted with a value system different from ours, is to begin an argument. It seems, at times, as if we must convince others that our approach to life is correct. If it is hard to listen to another point of view, we can see how impossible it is to enter another person's life orientation.

When Betty and Larry decided to move in together, Betty's parents were terribly upset. They refused to see how any good could come from living together. Betty pleaded with them for quite a while. Then, in a kind of desperation, she simply moved out of the house and in with Larry. An unsteady truce developed and, for a time, no progress was made on either side. After about six months, Betty came to talk with me about the situation.

"I think my parents are cruel," she burst out.

"I hope it's not cruelty. I hope they just have a hard time accepting your relationship with Larry."

"There is nothing immoral about what Larry and I are doing."

"I didn't mean to say there was. I just wanted to say that you and Larry have attitudes different from your parents."

"I don't see why they can't let us live our life the way we want to live it."

"I don't see how they can stop you."

"What do you mean?"

"You're living with Larry the way you want to, aren't you?"

"Yes, but they're sitting at home judging us. I want them to quit judging us."

"It might help if you stopped judging them."

"What?"

"Well, you're asking them to let you live your life the way you want to. I'm just asking you to let them have their attitudes."

"Oh?"

"Yeah. You want them to accept your moral code. Suppose you lead the way by letting them have their moral code?"

"I never thought about that."

"I wish you would. Once you quit asking your parents to approve your life, you will relieve yourself of a lot of anxiety."

The parent-child example may be extreme. Yet it does point up dramatically how blocked we can be to the viewpoint of another person. Betty was so anxious about her own situation that she demanded her parents' approval. It never dawned on her that her parents also had their point of view. It was all they could do to accept the fact that Betty and Larry lived together. To ask them also to approve the morality of the relationship was too much. They needed to be accepted in their attitude just as much as Betty needed acceptance in hers.

It might seem cruel to ask Betty to accept her parents' attitude toward the unmarried relationship. Yet that is what she must do if she is to grow close to them. She will begin to understand her parents when she is willing to understand their attitude. She does not need to accept their attitude or believe as they do. But she must let her parents have their attitudes before she will begin to understand them.

Fascinating

Listening to other people is a most difficult thing to do. Our mind says that shouldn't be so. Yet our experience tells us that it is. No resolution to pay more attention to others has any lasting effect. Even when listening is in our own best interests, we can still remain blocked from serving those interests. Most of us have sincerely tried, on one occasion or another, to listen and try to see the world from another person's point of view. Such attempts usually fall short of our expectations.

Before we will ever be able to listen to others, we need to develop a significant change of attitude. We have to begin by finding other people fascinating. For most of us this will be difficult. Even when we know people who are endlessly fascinating, we fail to give them our attention. We have to change this. We must genuinely want to learn about people the way we might want to learn about the stock market, the sports world, the fashion news, or current events. We must be willing to put time and effort into learning about people.

It is not enough to guess about people's attitudes and outlooks. We must want to learn firsthand what interests them, why they are interested, how they view the world, and what values are important to them. Only real interest will allow us to listen. If we are pretending to be interested, our attempts to hear others will fail.

Carl was about ready to move out on Debbie when he first talked to me. After nearly three years with Debbie, he was beginning to lose interest in her. What I found out, after he talked for a while, was that Carl knew very little about Debbie. They had a lot of fun together, shared many common interests, and even liked each other. In spite of their apparent compatibility, however, they knew each other only superficially.

The second time Carl saw me things had changed dramatically. "We finally talked," he said.

"How did it go?"

"It was fantastic. Debbie had been wanting to talk to me but was too scared. You know something? She is some girl."

"In what way?"

"In every way. You would be surprised at some of the things she has been thinking."

"I suppose I would be. Obviously you were."

"Debbie is really sensitive. She feels everything so deeply. I never dreamed she was so affected by things."

"I was afraid you didn't know her too well."

"I'll be honest with you. I was angry the first time you said that to me. But now that I know what you mean I am stunned."

"Stunned?"

"I just can't believe I lived with Debbie for three years and never got to know her."

"Just be glad you began before it was too late."

"Boy, I'll say. A few weeks ago we were about to end our relationship. Now it seems as though we are just beginning."

The world is filled with couples like Debbie and Carl who live together without knowing one another. In some cases, this attitude continues through silver and golden wedding anniversaries. Many couples marry, raise a family, grow old, and die without ever knowing one another. A sad commentary on our inability to listen to one another.

The saddest part of the Carl and Debbie story is the lack of fascination it implies. Carl was never sufficiently interested in Debbie to break through his inability to listen. For three years, he let his indifference rule his life with Debbie. He let himself be compatible but never once gave in to fascination.

Make It Worthwhile

Those who move in together do not sign a contract promising to listen to each other. Even couples who are close rarely express the need for listening. Yet that need for listening penetrates every relationship. The less couples listen to one another, the more the need is felt. At the root of most separations is the pressure nonlistening brings to a relationship. Listening draws couples close to one another, and lack of listening drives them apart.

There are couples, married and unmarried, who learn the art of nonlistening. They failed to listen to each other when they first met and will not be listening to each other the day they die. They simply decided, somewhere along the line, that they were not going to ask for emotional companionship. So they live with one another as emotional strangers. There may be a kind of physical compatability implicit in such relationships, but there is no sharing.

This book is directed at those who are

looking for more than a roommate. I assume there is a desire, within those couples who read this book, to share intimately with a partner. For such couples, listening is crucial. Listening is a prerequisite to emotional sharing. There is no way to guess the emotional inner life of a partner. We can learn only by listening. Those who listen are in a position to grow close. Those who make substitutions for listening are already beginning the separation process.

When Linda talked to me, she was moved emotionally. There were tears in her eyes when she told me about Dick.

"I've never met anyone like him."

"Hey, what are you crying about?"

"It's just that I'm so happy."

"Those are happy tears, then. Where are they coming from?"

"I guess I never thought it would happen to me. I found someone I can really love."

"That's great. You must have been awfully afraid of ending up an old maid."

"No, I knew I could find someone to marry. It's just that I wanted more than that."

"More than that?"

"Yes! I wanted to find someone I could open up to completely. I didn't want to marry just anyone. I wanted someone I could grow close to and really care about."

"That kind of love doesn't happen very often, does it?"

"No. I look around and see all the married people who are just existing with each other and I get scared. I think maybe that will happen to me."

"But now you have Dick."

"Oh, yes! It's like a dream come true. At first it seemed as if Dick was just another smooth talker. But now I know differently."

"What made the difference?"

"Dick and I have never been together that we haven't shared a part of ourselves. I don't mean we get morbid every time we are together, but we are almost always intimate and personal."

"You enjoy hearing about him?"

"I love it. Hearing Dick talk about himself is like being on an adventure. There are so many new and different aspects to his personality."

"And he wants to know about you?"

"He really does. I can tell. He wants to know about all the things no one else ever seemed interested in. At times, it's hard to know what I enjoy most—talking or listening."

"That sounds like the beginning of a fantastic relationship."

"It is. I'm just sure of it."

This early enthusiasm did not sustain itself indefinitely. Like every other couple, Dick and Linda had some difficult times in their relationship. Yet, the early attitudes did predict success. Underlying even the most difficult times was an intense interest in one another. They really liked to be with each other, and hearing about one another was always new and exciting. That bond grew strong and kept them close even when they were in conflict. Years after that first enthusiasm, Linda could say, "I still enjoy it when Dick talks about himself. It's always like meeting a brand new person."

I'm Talking to You 5

In the last chapter, we talked about listening and its importance. Now we can turn our attention to the other crucial element in communication—expressing our feelings.

When the importance of expressing feeling is mentioned, people often begin talking about the extremes. They will say things like, "If I told my boss what I think about him, I would probably be fired," or, "I don't want to go around crying all the time." The anger and tears such people are afraid to express are rarely spontaneous feelings. Severe emotion of this kind usually results from repressing feelings over a period of time. But by expressing them spontaneously, we can reduce the chance of emotional extremes.

The feelings that are the subject of this chapter are the emotions that often affect us during the average day. For example, we might be irritated by one person who talks too long when we are in a hurry. By contrast, a friend might please us by a kind word or a bit of praise. In both cases, the emotions only touch us lightly. We could keep these subtle reactions to ourselves and probably not be greatly affected by our concealment. At the same time, however, our communication with the people involved would be seriously damaged.

When it came to expressing his feelings, Jeff was no better and no worse than most young men his age. Yet he found it almost impossible to come right out and tell Patty, the young woman he was living with, how much he loved her.

"Sometimes the words get right up to the tip of my tongue and I still can't get them out," he told me.

"I think I know what you mean."

"It's not that I don't feel deeply for Patty. I do. There are times when I feel so close to her I get choked up. But it's almost impossible to tell her that."

"Do you know why?"

"I think so. It's my family. We just never told each other how we felt. I don't remember anyone ever saying, 'I love you.' It was there. There was lots of love in our family; but we just never talked about it."

"So with that background, it's hard for you to express your feelings."

"Wait a minute. I didn't tell you that story as an excuse."

"I didn't take it that way, either. It's just that when someone is raised in an atmosphere where feelings are rarely expressed, the difficulties are compounded."

"That doesn't mean I'm saying, 'My parents

are responsible.' I don't blame my parents for the way I am."

"I'm glad. Your parents can be a reason you find it hard to express your feelings. But they will never be an excuse."

Those who hear our words without hearing our feelings are getting only half the message. Jeff was not telling Patty the full story of his feeling for her. She might be able to guess how he felt about her. In fact, she probably did know, in view of Jeff's background, that his love was deeper than he could express. Yet the best understanding on Patty's part could not change the fact. Jeff was not communicating all of himself to Patty.

I Don't Understand

It might be important to pause here and look a little more carefully at what we mean when we say, "express your feelings." As was already mentioned, some people interpret the word "feeling" as extreme emotion—shouting and tears. Still others, reacting to the word, think of problems. To express their feelings, these people think they must reveal personal problems. One woman said to me, "How else do you get close to anyone if you don't tell them about your personal problems?"

No one would deny that talking about personal problems with friends brings you closer to them. Yet, this is not the only way to express feelings or, for that matter, to grow close to others. Expressing feelings is a much broader concept. "Feelings," as one friend put it, "are all those things I would rather not say." That definition may be crude and a bit simplistic, but it is fairly accurate.

By defining feelings as "those things I would rather not say," my friend was touching directly on the embarrassment that always surrounds a feeling. Whether they are affectionate impulses pulling us toward someone, or hostile emotions driving us away, feelings are always embarrassing. If we search for the reason, we would probably not find an answer. In fact, we are fortunate to recognize our feelings when they happen. And the best way to identify them is to notice "those things I would rather not say."

One young lady talked to me about some feelings she had not expressed to her lover. She was terrified that Ken would discover that she had, many years earlier, lived with Matt, a fellow she was then in love with. We talked about the matter for some time. I was surprised she felt so strongly about revealing her previous relationship. I could not believe Ken would be upset over something that had occurred so long ago. As we talked on, it became clear that Bev also thought Ken would not be greatly disturbed by knowing about Matt. That did not change her attitude, however. She said, "Even if I know Ken would not be upset, I would still be afraid to tell him about Matt."

It was two years before I heard from Bev again. This time she sent me a letter. Her letter made it seem as if we were just picking up the conversation where we had left off. She said, *"I wish I could see your face when you read that I told Ken that I had lived with someone else long before I met him. It was just as you said it would be. He wasn't the least bit upset. He was con-*

cerned that I needed to keep the truth from him, but he said, 'I love you just the same as always, maybe even more.' When I heard Ken say that, I felt an enormous relief.

"I know if I were there, you would probably ask why the whole thing was so hard for me to say. I have thought and thought about that. Especially since I talked to Ken I have wondered what was bothering me. I haven't come up with any answers. I could probably make up a reason for my fear. But inside I would know my reason didn't explain my reaction. I guess I will never know why I was so embarrassed. Maybe it really isn't very important."

There was no objective reason to explain why Bev had to tell Ken about Matt. Ken's attitudes were not greatly changed once he knew Bev had lived with someone else. Bev herself did not move in some new direction after she revealed her secret. The only important change was within Bev. There was some need, inside Bev, to reveal her relationship with Matt. She was pestered by her need for over two years. Then, when she could no longer stand the tension, she talked to Ken.

Feelings are like that—one part of us wants to say something, and another part of us is embarrassed by what we want to say. Important feelings are usually surrounded by severe embarrassment. In the case of Bev, the importance was not external and objective. The reason Bev needed to reveal her feelings was internal and largely mysterious. The best way to know the feeling was important was to notice the embarrassment surrounding it. Look for embarrassment and you will usually find a feeling. As my friend said, "Feelings are all those things I would rather not say."

Don't Hurt Me

It is not surprising that feelings are difficult to understand and to recognize. There is no neat definition that tells us exactly what a feeling is. We rather begin to recognize feelings by noticing their effects. For example, we identify some feelings when we associate them with embarrassment. We will recognize others when we learn to distinguish feelings from large bursts of emotion.

And inevitably, any expression of feeling leaves us vulnerable. If we say to someone, "I really enjoy being with you," that other person can hurt us deeply just by not saying anything. The defenselessness we suffer in that kind of situation can be shattering.

We are particularly vulnerable when we express emotions that might hurt another's feelings. There is a thin line between using a feeling to blame someone, and expressing the same feeling to draw close to someone. For this reason, the words we choose to express these feelings are of crucial importance.

If we feel irritable with a person who dominates the conversation, for example, we can accuse him by saying, "You haven't got enough sense to know when to stop talking." Such an attack is bound to make the compulsive talker defensive, and end any hope for communication. If we decide to express our feelings without attacking the talker, however, we have a good chance of establishing communication. If our emotion is impatience, we might say, "After you've talked for a while, I begin to get impatient." This second statement is not a direct accusation. Yet this, too, is a dangerous approach because it leaves us vulnerable to the talker. He might very well tell us what we can do with our impatience. On the other hand, most sensitive people will recognize our vulnerability and respond positively. In fact, such a vulnerable statement is often the beginning of significant communication.

A number of years ago I was consulted by a young woman who was worried about her brother-in-law's drinking. I was particularly concerned because I knew all the people involved. Paul, the young man with the problem, had all the signs of alcoholism. Whether he had passed over the line from problem drinking into alcoholism could be debated. What could not be debated was the seriousness of the problem. Allison's eyes reflected her anxiety when she asked me, "What should I do?"

"What do you think you should do?"

"Well, I think I should say something that would make him stop. But I don't know what that would be."

"Do you honestly think there is something you can say to make Paul stop drinking?"

"No, not really. But I can't just stand by while he drinks himself to death."

"You make it sound as if there are only two alternatives."

"What do you mean?"

"You are saying that you must either say something to make Paul stop drinking, or you have to stand by and watch him kill himself."

"I'm not sure I understand you."

"Let's turn the situation around for a minute. Put yourself in Paul's place. You have let your drinking get the best of you. You can't control how much you drink. Now I come along and say, 'Allison, you've got to stop drinking. You are ruining your health, hurting your family, and making life miserable for everyone.' How would you react?"

"I see what you mean. I would really be angry with you."

"Suppose under the same circumstances I didn't say anything about your drinking. How would you react?"

"I guess I would assume you didn't care very much about me. Well—what would *you* do in a case like that?"

"I would express my feelings to you, Allison. I would probably say something like, 'Your drinking is your own business, Allison. I don't pretend to have anything to say about it. I just want you to know that the way things are going now I am concerned. I am deeply troubled for you and wish there were something I could do to help.' "

"I see. I see. That way you aren't making any demands on me. You are telling me how you feel and I am free to respond or not respond. Do you think that would work with Paul?"

"There is no way to say for sure. Paul just might tell you to mind your own business."

"That would be awful. If I opened myself up like that and Paul told me to mind my own business, I would die."

"That's part of the risk you take. There is no way to avoid it."

Allison did finally approach Paul. As she

said later, "I left myself wide open." Fortunately, Paul responded. He had begun to despair over the lack of understanding he met on every hand. Lots of people were telling him to stop drinking, but few had shown real concern. Until Allison came along, no one had revealed any sensitivity to what he was going through. Allison's openness gave Paul a chance to express some of the confusion that had him in turmoil. Allison not only brought Paul immediate help but also opened him to future communication.

Both Sides Now

It is as if we have two messages for people. One comes from our intellect, the other from our emotions. We most often express the thoughts that develop in our intellect. Even when we do express our emotions, we have a way of trying to intellectualize them. For example, we have all heard people say, "I don't know why I'm angry with you," as if emotion is only legitimate when some reason explains its existence. Few of us can say, "I'm really angry at you right now," without quickly trying to explain our anger.

The message that comes from emotions is most often expressed as a feeling. Most of us are so uncomfortable about our feelings that we find it difficult even to identify them. It takes some people a long period of reflection before they realize they have feelings. They are so used to hiding from those embarrassing movements, they become unaware of them.

Communication will never be complete until we are able to express both of our messages. If we continue to reveal our intellectual message without expressing the emotional message, others will never know what is happening inside of us. They will obviously have a distorted picture of us. That distortion will certainly make true communication impossible.

Mary was just about to leave Art when she came to see me. They had been living together for about two years, but those years were not what Mary had expected. By the time she talked to me, she was fed up. "I just decided that Art is no damn good," she said, with obvious disgust.

"Bring me up to date, Mary. Why are you so upset?"

"It's no one reason. It's just that Art is obviously not interested in me."

"He's been living with you for two years, hasn't he?"

"That's just his sex trip. He really doesn't care about me."

"Now, wait a minute. Just what makes you so sure he doesn't care about you?"

"For one thing, he never says he cares. I can't remember the last time he said 'I love you.' "

"That doesn't mean the feeling isn't there."

"If he felt it he would say it."

"I suppose he ought to express his feelings, but then most of us do a poor job of it."

"Well, I always tell Art *my* feelings."

"I'll have to question that."

"Question what?"

"I wonder if you really express your feelings to Art."

"What do you mean?"

"My guess is you never told Art you need him to express his feelings more."

"I don't get it."

"You said you always tell Art your feelings. I'll bet you never told him what you just told me."

"What's that?"

"I'll bet you never told him you want him to express his feelings more."

"I hate to admit it, but you're right."

"You can't expect him to guess what is bothering you."

"I know."

"It's really embarrassing to let other people know your needs. But since you are asking Art to express his feelings, you ought to express yours first."

When Mary finally did ask Art to express his feelings more often, he was relieved. He knew something was bothering her, but never guessed what it was. He had imagined the worst. The truth was mostly a release from his fears. That did not make it any easier for him to express himself. He still had to struggle for expression. But the struggle was eased when he was no longer distracted by other, more serious doubts.

All of Me

We will only communicate ourselves to others when we learn to blend thoughts and feelings. Inside our own mind there is no sharp distinction between what we think and what we feel. Even our reactions to business, politics, and weather are a mixture of thoughts and emotion. Certainly the more significant elements of our life are filled with emotion as well as ideas. Our attempts to pick out our thoughts and strip them of feeling before we communicate can only falsify what is actually happening inside of us.

It is not easy for most of us to simultaneously

communicate thoughts and feelings. We rarely encounter people who express emotion in union with their ideas. In fact, most of us have been trained to avoid any expression of feeling. As children, we were bombarded with commands like, "Act like a man and quit pouting," or, "Stop that crying, or I'll give you something to cry about." So that by now most of us have very negative attitudes toward emotion.

These attitudes are unfortunate. For it is only by expressing our total self—thoughts and feelings—that we will be able to draw close to others. There is no such thing as intimacy without revealing the secret part of ourselves. We must lower the barriers we have erected between our inner selves and other people. Once another person sees how our thoughts intermingle with our feelings, that person will begin to see us as a human being like himself. Then we will be prepared for intimacy.

Naturally, the expression of self is crucial to any communion between those who live together. Two people who decide to live together, but continue to hide from one another, can never experience intimacy. A countless number of couples living together refuse to share their emotional life. Their struggle for intimacy is futile. They can work together, play together, make love together, and still remain distant. Their refusal to share emotionally will make separation inevitable.

Time for Bed 6

There is one fear, implicit in the unmarried relationship, that deserves special mention—fear of sexual inadequacy. Most of us feel that we are inadequate sexually. The media contribute to this. Our movies, television shows, magazines, and best-selling novels suggest an unreasonable ideal. Without ever saying so directly, they hint that the sexually adequate man can come to erection in a matter of moments. The media-woman appears ready for orgasm at any time.

Books, magazines, and movies also dwell on the problem of impotence. The man or woman with a blocked sex drive is an object of fascination. Many plots focus on the unfortunate person who has lost the ability to perform sexually. Sometimes the problem is blamed on family background. In other cases the marriage relationship will be cited as the cause of the problem. At still other times the impotence appears hereditary. In each case, however, the author appears preoccupied with impotence.

Such extremes exist in the real world outside the media. There are people so sexually potent it is overwhelming. At the same time, others must deal with the problem of impotence. The media are not lying. The media fail only because they ignore the space between potency and impotence. That space is where most of us exist. The most enthusiastic, virile, and stimulated male can suddenly lose his erection. A woman who is passionate, receptive, and energetic can turn cold in a moment. Sometimes we can explain the strange turns our sexual drives take. At other times, no explanation seems adequate.

After class one day Mark stopped me and asked if we could talk. He was obviously reluctant to get to the point. So we spent some time chatting about the class and other things. Finally, after about ten minutes, Mark said, "This isn't what I came to talk about."

"I didn't think so."

"I don't know how to say this. I guess—well, I'm worried about sex."

"I think we all are, but what's your worry?"

"It's my relationship with Sandy. I'm afraid something is wrong."

"Why do you say that?"

"Well, before we moved in together, I wanted sex every time we got together. We were always looking for some corner where we could have sex. I just couldn't get enough."

"And now things are different."

"That's right. We've only been living together about two months and my attitude is starting to change."

"What is your new attitude like?"

"During the last week I haven't wanted to

touch Sandy. And I mean touch her. Not just avoid sex. I haven't wanted to touch her."

"Have you stopped having sex during this last week?"

"Oh, no. I couldn't do that. I wouldn't want her to know how I feel. It would kill her."

"Doesn't forcing sex just make it that much harder for you?"

"It sure does. It scares me, too. I'm afraid there must be something wrong with me. I mean, normal healthy people don't just stop wanting sex."

Mark was convinced there was something wrong with him sexually. As I discovered later, he was even more frightened than I realized. He was a victim of the usual myth that any lack of sexual enthusiasm is a disaster. He was even afraid to mention his attitude to Sandy. This meant his fears were compounded by his pretense.

It is easy to sympathize with Mark. We all have our sexual doubts. We worry about failures, lack of enthusiasm, and attitude changes. The last person we want to tell is our partner. We feel that such a revelation would upset our lover, even make that lover wonder about us. So we hide our disturbance and let it fester. Then what begins as a minor irritation can, in time, grow into a major obstacle in our relationship.

What Are You Afraid Of?

When it comes to sex, there are apparently an unlimited number of things couples are afraid to express to one another. It sometimes seems almost anything connected with sex can become repressed out of embarrassment. I have known people who were afraid to say to their lover, "I wish we didn't have sex so often." Others are just as uneasy about saying, "I'm not getting enough sex." Another frequent cause of embarrassment is the desire to say, "I just don't enjoy sex as I used to." A lot of people are unable to admit, "I am getting plenty of sex but still don't seem satisfied."

Most of us can find plenty of reasons for not expressing our fears to a partner. Among other things, we "don't want to hurt" our lover, are afraid "it might make matters worse," or "just can't bring" ourselves "to do it." In most cases such reasons are real. We really do fear hurting a partner or making matters worse.

The truth is that sexual problems are most embarrassing. Something about the subject makes any deficiency seem more serious than it is. Even in a close relationship we can be embarrassed by sexual problems. Sometimes it is even more difficult to discuss a sexual fear with a lover than with anyone else.

Kathie, a friend of mine, found it easier to talk about her sexual fears with me than with Don, the fellow she was living with.

"I am so afraid that I'm not satisfying Don," she told me with a great deal of embarrassment.

"Is that what Don says?"

"No, Don hasn't said anything yet."

"Then why are you worried?"

"That's just it, I don't know *why* I'm worried. I just know that I'm scared to death."

"Couldn't you talk to Don about your fear? Maybe you're all worked up over nothing."

"No, I couldn't possibly talk to Don. That scares me more than anything."

"But you and Don are close, aren't you?"

"Oh, yes. We are closer than most couples who live together. Maybe that's part of the problem."

"Part of the problem?"

"Yeah. For some reason it's harder to talk about my sexual fears with Don than with other close friends."

"Really?"

"Yes. I can open up to close friends. But somehow, even the thought of telling Don about my fear that I'm not satisfying him just terrifies me."

"I guess I do understand that feeling."

"Maybe sex is too important. If Don knew how sexually inadequate I feel, I'm afraid he might lost interest in me."

There was a lot of truth in what Kathie was saying. We all know that revealing sexual feelings is embarrassing. That embarrassment is compounded, however, when we are revealing our failings to someone close. It is as if the risk is greatest when the friendship is most important. Our mind says this is not the way things should be. Our emotions tell us the real truth, however. The fear of revealing sexual fears to a lover can be the most serious fear we ever face.

What's Wrong?

It is crucial for a couple living together to discuss their sexual difficulties. Just because a couple is close does not free them from the fears and doubts that accompany sexual expression. Naturally, all that was said in the previous chapter about expressing fears to a partner holds for sexual fears. There is a special reason, however, for expressing sexual fears to a partner.

More often than not, sexual fears reflect relationship fears. The fear that I am not performing properly can often reflect a fear that I am not loving my partner enough. The fear of sexual aggressiveness can arise from a concern over becoming domineering in a relationship. Most couples who have grown close will recognize the symbolism that sex can play in a relationship. The expression of the symbolic sexual doubts can open a discussion of other doubts that are causing relationship problems.

Too much can be made of the symbolism that sex plays in a relationship. Some pyschologists draw detailed conclusions just by listening to the symptoms of sexual inadequacy. Such particularized conclusions are misguided. Yet, every couple would do well to pay close attention to their sexual fears and doubts. There are times when such fears carry no further meaning. At other times, expressing a sexual fear can help a couple uncover a serious problem that has been straining their relationship.

Bruce was slightly overwhelmed when he found there was more to a sexual incompatibility than he had imagined. As he said, "I knew Dianne's passive attitude bothered me, but I never knew there was more to it than that."

"Her passive attitude?"

"Yes. Any time we made love, it was up to me to do most of the work. For the most part, she just lay there."

"I don't suppose you ever talked to her about it."

"Not until last week. Finally, I couldn't take it any longer. I just told her she was relying too much on me."

"What did she say?"

"That's the strange part. At first she didn't realize I was talking about making love. She started to defend herself. She told me how much time she puts into cleaning our apartment, into the planning of the meals, and stuff like that."

"And—"

"And it came to me in a flash. Her passive attitude had to do with more than sex. It was a kind of role she was playing. All at once I realized she was passive in everything, not just in love-making."

"So did you finally talk about it?"

"We really talked it out. Here we had been living together for nearly two years and we never talked about the roles we were playing."

"Did you discover you were playing a role, too?"

"Oh, yeah. I've been the big decision-maker. Dianne said I would never let her make any real decisions. No wonder she became passive."

"So you were bothering her as much as she was bothering you."

"That's right. Maybe even more. In any event, we are trying to break out of our roles."

"How are you doing that?"

"By changing roles every now and then. On a given day, she will do my chores and I will take over hers."

"That sounds pretty good."

"It is."

"Did you also work on your love-life?"

"We didn't have to. Once we had our long talk, things also started to improve in bed. We just naturally seemed to solve our problems there, too."

It would be hard to say whether Dianne's

passive attitude began in bed or in her role with Bruce. It's probably not very important. The important truth is that Dianne's passivity reflected itself in every part of her life. A change in one part of that attitude changed Dianne completely. The same was true of Bruce. Once he changed the dominant tone in his relationship with Dianne, he changed his entire attitude toward her.

By being sensitive to the symbols involved in love-making, a couple can begin to see their relationship more clearly. It is somehow easier to see aggressiveness, passivity, hostility, or tenderness in love-making than it is to see those qualities as part of a relationship. In our day-to-day relating, we unwittingly conceal our troubling feelings from our partner. Soon a disturbing attitude can be accepted as part of a relationship, and left unquestioned. The best way to uncover that disturbing element is to discover how it is distracting us from our love-making.

I'd Rather Not Say

No discussion of revealing sexual fear would be complete without mentioning the fear of confessing a second love. Even in the closest relationships, partners can find themselves attracted to someone else. Even though one has no intention of becoming interested, the attraction can lead to deep involvement. There is nothing we are so apt to hide from a partner as the second love. At the same time, nothing is so important to discuss as the second love. With serious discussion of the outside relationship, there is some hope of reaching a solution. The solution may be separation or it may be staying together to work things through. But no solution can be reached as long as the second relationship remains secret.

Some shrink from the thought of mentioning an affair to their partner. This is understandable. Secrecy seems intimately linked to the very concept of an affair. Old taboos restrain couples from revealing outside attractions to each other. Yet such taboos suggest a rigid form of relating. They hardly apply to the open relationship most people living together profess to practice.

Those who enter the living-together relationship normally do so in order to have more freedom than in marriage. As one young woman said to me, "I never want to get married. It's too much like being trapped." That freedom to separate also contains an obligation. The obligation demands honesty and openness from both partners. Any danger to the relationship must be shared. One partner does not have the right to conceal a serious threat.

Molly seemed to feel she was perfectly justified in having an affair without telling Jay. She said, "I think it is best for both of us that Jay never finds out about Wayne."

"Don't you think Jay has some rights, too?"

"If Jay found out about Wayne, he would only be hurt."

"I'm sure he would be hurt, but I still think he has a right to know the truth."

"Why?"

"Well, it's his relationship, too. I think he has a right to know what you are doing with it."

"I don't see why you want me to hurt him."

"Hurt him! It would be impossible for you to hurt him more than you're hurting him right now."

"Oh, be serious."

"I am being serious. If I were Jay, I would much rather be told about Wayne than be left to wonder."

"Really?"

"You bet. If you want to know the truth, I think you are just afraid to face Jay with the truth."

"That may be true."

"About the hardest thing in the world is to tell someone about a second lover. I know I would never want that job."

"You're right. I don't even like to think about it."

"I suspect you could look a little more honestly at your decision to hide the truth from Jay."

"Suppose I do tell Jay about my relationship with Wayne. What would that prove?"

"It might not prove anything. On the other hand, a long talk with Jay just might lead you two back together again."

"That would never happen."

"Even if that's true, I still think Jay has a right to hear about Wayne from you. You know he's going to hear about him eventually. I think you owe it to Jay to tell him about Wayne yourself."

Telling someone about a second lover is a terrible ordeal. The emotions involved can be overwhelming. The pain of working through all those emotions is something most of us would rather avoid. Yet the only healthy way to deal with the pain is to look at it directly. Each day we wait to talk about the second lover only increases the pain.

Often no fault is involved in a second relationship. Such things happen without any deliberation. It would be foolish to point the finger of blame when we become involved with someone else. That lack of blame does not diminish our responsibility, however. Even when the second relationship "just happens," we are still responsible to our partner. We must share the truth honestly and openly.

Three's a Crowd

All the talk about second lovers might seem to overlook new patterns that are developing in relationships. Group sex relationships are being tested regularly. In the case of many "swingers," the goal seems to be to find out how many different people can have sex simultaneously. At the same time, more serious attempts at group relating are being explored. While many such attempts do fail, there are a lot of successful experiments.

There is one great difference between the affair and successful group sex experiments. Healthy group sex experiments are based on honesty and openness. That openness is in sharp contrast to the secrecy intrinsic to the affair. It is not uncommon in a commune, for example, for members to devote a significant amount of time to talking through relationship-problems that develop. More often than not, successful group-relating is based on a schedule that has time set aside for everyone to express feelings.

We return to a recurring theme—communication. The open and honest expression of feeling is important to successful relating. For those who choose to live together, communication is crucial. Without any legal ties holding a couple together, the quality of their

communication often makes the difference between staying together and separating. Even
more important, however, healthy communication can make the difference between happiness and misery in a relationship.

I'm not Jealous 7

Jealousy is a serious problem for couples living together. In fact, it may be the most frequent cause of discord between unmarried couples. Sometimes there is good reason for the jealousy. At other times, the jealous response has no real cause. In both situations, however, the problem is real. Jealousy puts most relationships under strain.

Just a few years ago, jealousy was understood to be part of the intimate relationship. The wife who discovered her husband was having an affair was expected to sue for divorce. A man often took a gun after his wife's lover. Everyone understood. Maybe more than merely understanding, they expected the jealous response. Rarely did anyone regret showing jealousy. People were more likely to wonder about a lack of jealousy than they were to question jealous passion.

Times have changed. A new ethic suggests

jealousy is something evil. I have heard people say, "I hate myself when I am jealous," "Jealousy is always destructive," and "My jealousy is vicious and evil." Most couples now assume that the jealous response only suggests how immature and self-centered they are.

One recent classroom discussion stands out, not because it was unique, but rather because it was so typical. One young man was berating himself for his jealousy. He said, "I know I'm not supposed to get jealous when Jan is spending the night with another guy. But I just can't help it."

"Have you talked to her about it?" a young woman asked sympathetically.

"Yes, we have talked and talked," Tom said with a bit of sadness.

"What does she say?"

"She just says she needs her freedom. She said she wants to be free to see other guys."

"She's right, you know," an older male student said from the back of the room. "If you start telling her who she can see and who she can't see, you might as well be married."

"Yeah, I know. I hate myself. I hate being jealous. I just don't know what to do."

"Have you thought about seeing other gals?" another young woman inquired.

"I have. It just doesn't work. Jan is the only one I want to be with. Being with someone else just doesn't mean anything."

"You better be careful," warned another student. "My first wife left me because I started telling her to stop seeing other guys."

"That's what scares me," Tom said with obvious pain. "I think she's already thinking of moving out on me."

"Maybe you'd better play it cool for a while. Just stop talking about who she sees and who she doesn't see."

"I've been trying. Believe me, I've been trying. For about three months now, I haven't said anything. She has been seeing other guys and I haven't opened my mouth. But the pressure is getting to me. I just can't go on this way."

There was a pause around the room. No one seemed to know what to say next. Tom apparently violated all the accepted rules for the unmarried relationship. He was jealous. He wanted Jan all to himself. Jan's other relationships were bothering him and he could not change his attitude. Some students must have sympathized with Tom but no one said anything.

There are many reasons for the change in attitude toward jealousy. For one thing, many of these students saw their parents become victims to marriage commitments. They suffered because their parents lacked the freedom to end an unhappy relationship. They fear that sort of commitment. They value freedom and choice.

Obviously, jealousy is a force that limits freedom. The jealous instinct tends to restrict and to control. No wonder those in unmarried relationships can become terrified of their jealousy. They agreed to live together so they could avoid the restrictions of marriage. Yet even in the unmarried relationship, they find themselves being jealous. The emotional contradiction can be painful.

Try to Forget It

Many unmarried couples are disgusted by their own jealousy. They normally try to stamp out this response. Rarely do they think of letting their jealousy dissipate over a period of time. Most are too impatient for that. Their response is more likely to be, "I have to change. And I have to change now." Each jealous moment is considered a terrible burden.

An almost instinctive response to the jealous emotion is pretense. "If I can pretend I'm not jealous long enough," one young woman told me, "pretty soon my jealousy is gone." In another case, a young fellow goes out with other women when his partner is spending the night elsewhere. Many young people turn to smoking marijuana when they want to forget their jealousy. As another young man commented, "After a couple of joints, I forget where she is. Sometimes I don't even know where I am." There are, of course, a countless number of other distractions that are effective during a period of jealousy.

At times such diversions work. The jealous response can quickly subside during an athletic contest, a rock concert, or a pot party. Other times, nothing works. The more we try to forget our jealousy, the worse it gets. Even in the midst of wild diversion, jealousy can preoccupy and poison us. We do not know why diversions sometimes work and other times fail. A lot of theories could be advanced, but none gives us any certitude. We can be certain of only one thing. There are times when no diversion will distract us from our jealousy.

Robin had to find out personally that there is no certain escape from jealousy. When she told me her story, she was practically in tears. Her relationship had obviously cost her a lot of pain. There was no way she could hide that pain.

"When we moved in together, I really wanted Gene to be free," she told me. "I wanted to let him see anyone at any time. I wanted him to have women friends as well as men friends."

"What happened?"

"My attitude started to change. I became jealous of his friends. Whenever he was late coming home, I would get nervous and sometimes even a little frantic."

"Why was that? Did he start to stay away for longer periods?"

"Oh, no, just the opposite. He tried to be home when he said he would be home. He even dropped a lot of his friends."

"Then I don't understand why you were jealous."

"Neither do I. All I knew was I couldn't bear to think of his having fun with anyone else."

"Did you talk to Gene about all this?"

"No, I suppose I should have, but I didn't. No, I tried to hide from my feelings."

"Hide from your feelings?"

"Yes. Every time I got upset worrying about where Gene was, I would turn on the television set. I didn't care what was on. I would watch anything to get rid of those horrible feelings."

"Did it work?"

"At first it did. For a while I could lose myself for long periods of time. Then, it didn't work any more. After a while, I couldn't distract myself. No matter what I was doing, I was thinking about Gene and wondering where he was and what he was doing. It was awful."

"I don't understand why you didn't talk to Gene about all this."

"What could he do? It wasn't his fault. And I was afraid if he knew what a bitch I was becoming, he would leave me."

"Well, what did happen, then?"

"The worst. I kept hiding my feelings for months. Then one evening I blew up. Some little thing—I can't even remember what it was—rubbed me the wrong way and I exploded. I screamed at Gene, made all kinds of accusations, and just abused him something awful."

"Oh, that is bad. Could Gene handle it?"

"No! No one could handle all that. He just got angry and started shouting back at me. Poor guy didn't even know what it was all about."

"Did it all end right away?"

"No, we hung on for several more weeks. But we both knew it was over. We had too far to go. There was really little chance we could get together after that argument. There were just too many misunderstandings."

Robin made a basic mistake in her attempts to hide from her jealousy. She thought she could make the jealousy disappear. At first, this seemed to be happening. Then, even Robin knew her jealousy was getting worse. Yet she gave in to her fear that Gene would leave her if she let him know how upset she really was. So the jealousy festered and grew. Before long her emotions were so strong they could not help but destroy the relationship. Finally, there was no hope of repairing the damage that Robin's aggravated emotions had caused.

We may not have experienced this same destructive force. Yet most of us know the potency of a repressed emotion. We know what it is to be unable to distract ourselves from anger, fear, or jealousy. When the movie, magazine, or drink fails to do its job, we can find ourselves even more disturbed later on. The minor upset, the troubling moment, the disturbing glance can become a major distraction.

There are many ways to handle jealousy. At times, distractions work wonders. But if distractions are failing and we continue to use them, our use can become an abuse. That is dangerous. Distractions have a vicious way of turning around and punishing those who abuse them.

Don't Get Involved

As the ideal of nonjealousy grows, more people are going to try to end their jealous feelings. Those who become too preoccupied with their goal will find themselves standing aloof from their partner. One way of avoiding jealousy is to become uninvolved. This process can happen unconsciously. Many people who pride themselves on never getting jealous are not aware that they have become indifferent. They control their emotional involvement so that jealousy will not disturb their relationship. Those who are most effective not only eliminate their jealousy but also every other emotion.

Only those who risk revealing their emotions can become intimate with one another. As long as couples remain superficial in their communication, they will never experience the emotional bond that draws two people close. The person who is in horror over jealous feelings is at least honest enough to recognize inner emotion. Those who pretend to be unaffected by such turmoil also refuse to be touched emotionally.

Not too long ago, a student gave me his journal-diary to read. In it he talked at length about the jealousy his partner felt toward him. At one point he said, *"Joyce is really upset about her jealousy. Sometimes I think she is more upset about it than I am. Whenever she sees me with Jill or Suzanne or any of the other gals at school, she gets really upset . . . . Then later she gets mad for being angry. Sometimes it's hard to tell whether she's mad at me or at herself."*

About three weeks later, Jim made this entry: *"Every time Joyce asks me if I get jealous, I say, 'No, I don't think I ever have.' What I never mention is the fact that she never has given me much reason to be jealous. And the few times I have felt a little jealous I don't mention. I'm not sure why I don't tell Joyce about my jealousy. I probably like it this way. As long as Joyce is mad at herself for being jealous, I feel a little superior."*

Less than two weeks after this entry, Jim made an important discovery. *"Boy, I really feel awful,"* he wrote. *"I think I understand why I don't get as jealous as Joyce. I think it's because I haven't let myself get as involved as she has. I suddenly realize how much she loves me. It was strange. Last night she said, 'Jim, I think I love you more than anyone else in the world,' and I couldn't say anything. I was just frozen. No wonder she gets jealous of me. She would really be hurt if I left her. And all the while I have been playing it cool. I was too afraid to really let myself get involved with Joyce."*

So many of us share Jim's fear. We would rather not let ourselves become involved. That means taking a chance. Once we open ourselves emotionally to another person we can be hurt. It is so much safer to remain distant and aloof. That way we will be less affected by any strain on the relationship. If we manage to keep our emotions under control, we can even avoid the curse of jealousy. Jealousy is not possible as long as we remain distant enough from the one who could cause us jealousy.

Just Be Yourself

We are a complex network of emotion and feeling. On any given day, we will experience an entire spectrum of emotion—a moment of sadness, a flash of anger, and a period of joy. These periods of emotion are maintained by a delicate balance. They arrive and depart in a sense of harmony. No period of sadness will last too long nor can we sustain a moment of pleasure by simple effort. A natural mechanism within our personality keeps our emotions in an overall balance.

Our goal is not to change our personalities. Rather it is to accept ourselves as the persons we are. We are a certain network of emotion and feeling. We react in certain ways when confronted with the circumstances of life. We must deal with an impulse that makes us upset, at times, with the persons we are. We put a lot of effort into trying to change our natural emotional responses. That energy might be better spent in trying to accept the reality of ourselves.

Jealousy is the case in point. There is no way we can radically change our jealous instincts. Any attempt to uproot jealousy from our lives is going to end in frustration. We would do better to accept jealousy as one part of our emotional self. There are times when we are jealous just as there are times when we are lonely, or sad, or depressed. There is nothing so horrible about experiencing times of jealousy. It is not the worst thing that can happen to us.

Lynne was a person who found it almost impossible to accept her jealousy. She struggled with herself for months trying to change her attitude toward Stan, the fellow she was living with. Naturally, I was surprised to see her so happy the day I met her in the drugstore.

"You certainly look a lot happier than the last time I saw you," I said.

"That's probably because I am a lot happier than last time we talked."

"What happened?"

"Well, you probably remember how jealous I was of Stan."

"How could I forget?"

"It was pretty bad, wasn't it?"

"Yes, it was. But tell me, what happened?"

"Well, I kept getting more and more angry with myself for being jealous. I just thought I was the ugliest, cruelest, most vicious person that ever lived."

"I remember that part."

"Well, I finally got so upset I couldn't handle it any more. I had to have a real heart-to-heart talk with Stan."

"How did Stan react?"

"He was wonderful. He said he didn't like it when I was jealous. But he also said that he didn't think my jealousy was as bad as I made it out to be."

"That's what I was trying to tell you."

"I know. That's what everyone has been trying to tell me. But I just couldn't hear it. Somehow Stan got through to me last night. I can't explain why but I finally realized that jealousy isn't the worst thing in the world."

"That's wonderful."

"You bet it is. Now when I'm jealous I know Stan understands. He doesn't like me to be jealous. I don't like to be jealous. But if it happens, it happens."

"And you can just let yourself be jealous."

"And I can just let myself be jealous."

Lynne had taken a big step toward self-acceptance. She had accepted her jealousy as part of herself. What neither of us knew was that this was just a first step. In the months that followed this conversation, she began to look more carefully at herself. She saw a lot of things she did not like. She had more anger than she thought was proper. She spent more time being depressed than seemed normal. She was even unhappy with the way she covered her emotion with a nervous laugh.

Lynne looked at each of these tendencies carefully and asked, "Is it all right? Is it all right to be angry, to be depressed, to cover emotion?" She was not able to think of any reason that she should hide any part of herself. She would rather not be angry, depressed, or lonely. Given the choice, she would change all these emotions. But since these emotions were really part of her, why should she be ashamed of them?

The change in Lynne continued to be dramatic. Each week found her happier with herself. As she said some time later, "I hardly ever get jealous any more. There are still times when it comes up. But I just say to Stan, 'You know, last night I started to get jealous of the long talk you had with that woman at the party.' Sometimes we talk about it. Sometimes we don't. Now jealousy is just another part of me. It's still an important part, but I don't treat it as if it was the only part."

A Sign of Affection

So far this chapter has suggested that jealousy is always negative. It is discussed as an emotion to endure, to eliminate, or to try to change. Most couples who live together put it into such categories. So it has been realistic until now to discuss it in such a context. Now that we have spent some time looking at the negative aspects of jealousy, we might consider some situations when jealousy leads to positive results.

For example, take the case of Grace, a woman of forty-five who told me the story of her jealous-free marriage. It was quite disturbing. A little wistfully she said, "Yes, I had the perfect attitude in my marriage. I told John he could have a relationship with anyone who attracted him. I told him I trusted him completely. And I did. I really believed John would never fall in love with another woman."

"What happened?"

"After nine years of marriage, he asked me for a divorce so he could marry my best friend."

"Really?"

"Oh, yes, really. I found out later that I had driven him away. I gave him every reason to believe I didn't care. He told me later he thought my career was more important to me than he was."

"And was that true?"

"No, it wasn't true. I was completely and totally in love with John. I was so much in love that I thought he must be bound to me in the same way."

"But he wasn't?"

"I'll never be sure. If he was, my matter-of-fact attitude drove him away."

Suggesting that jealousy is a sign of affection is a touchy business. In the most obvious way, jealousy does not express affection. Altruistic love always seeks the freedom of the loved one. When we are feeling most secure with ourselves, we want our partner to experience maximum freedom. We would always like to wish our lover expansion and growth. Jealousy, by contrast, demands restriction and control. It is never an expression of expansive love.

The ideal world would see us always wishing our lover the freedom to grow in other relationships. The real world finds us often feeling possessive toward the one we love. We may hate ourselves for such a feeling, but it is a part of our life. It is so much a part of even the best love relationships that its absence makes us wonder. A lack of jealousy can also indicate a lack of concern and love.

I never met Grace's husband so I can only speculate about his feelings. Yet I think it is fair to say that we all expect some jealousy from our partner. In the world of rich love, jealousy is inevitable. Once we open ourselves to another person, we fear the loss of that person.

We know that anyone who knows us intimately can make us jealous. We protect ourselves instinctively from that pain. When our partner does not exhibit some of the same jealousy, we begin to wonder. Are we really loved? Has our partner been honest with us? Doubt, rather than reassurance, can sometimes result from a complete absence of jealousy.

I Love All of You

A young man who was in an encounter group with me several years ago summed up the nature of love as well as anyone. "When I am with my girl," he said, "I never have the urge to be anything except myself. She never puts me under any pressure to play a role. I don't have to be a student, a lover, or even a man when I am with her. All she expects is that I be myself."

When asked about his feelings toward her, he said, "I feel the same about her. I only want her to be herself. I enjoy her more when she is happy, at ease, or even a little silly. But I would feel betrayed if she were to hide from me the person she happens to be at any given moment. I want to share her fear, her doubts, her anger, and her pain. Otherwise, I don't know how I could love her."

We all recognize our own desires in that statement. We want, more than anything else, to be accepted for ourselves. Particularly when we are troubled, depressed, or fearful, we want to know there is someone who cares. We don't want to have to pretend. We would rather not cover our turmoil. We want someone who will say, "It's all right to be fearful, confused, or angry. I don't want you to change. I just want you to be yourself. And no matter how upset you might be, I still love you. You see, I'm not in love with any part of you. I'm in love with you."

It is more difficult to turn that attitude around—particularly in the case of jealousy. We cannot so easily say, "I get jealous at times. I don't like it, but that's the way I am. I hope you can let me be jealous when those moods hit me. I know my moods will restrict and bind you at times and I don't want that. I wish I were never jealous. I wish I would never put any restrictions on you. But that's me. I hope our love will grow so that, as time goes by, I will be less jealous and restrictive. In the meantime, I hope you will let me be my jealous self when I need to, so that I won't have to pretend. I don't want to pretend. I love you too much for that."

Don't
Get
Mad 8

A young man in the back of the class remarked, "Every time I get upset with my old lady, I go out behind our place and chop down a tree. When I'm through I feel a lot better." Another fellow responded, "Does that work for you? I like to sit by myself and meditate. I can usually get over being angry in a short time." One young woman could hardly wait to get into the conversation. "When I get burned with the guy who lives with me, I just start running. Sometimes I run a mile or more before I finally cool off." An older student offered, "My favorite way to unwind is to take up my guitar and play. In no time, I'm lost to the music and can't even remember what made me mad."

This discussion and a lot of others like it can go on for hours without anyone saying, "When I get angry with the one I'm living with, I like to sit down and let my partner know just what is making me angry." There seems to be an assumption among couples who live together that anger is a terrible threat to their relationship. It is as if most people find it impossible to think of anger as anything but destructive. They seem to think it must be avoided at all costs.

The truth is that the repression of anger is likely to hurt a relationship more than the expression of it ever can. By trying to hide anger, we force our partner to guess what is wrong with us. Our partner would have to be pretty insensitive to be unaware we were holding something back. Little movements, involuntary reactions, tone of voice all give away our mood. The problem is that such reactions do not reveal *what* is making us angry. Our partner only knows we are upset and is left to wonder why. We all know how disturbing it is to try to guess what is bothering someone. It is unfair to put that burden on anyone, especially on a lover.

We can find any number of reasons for not expressing the anger that is bursting to come into the open. The young woman who seemed to personify all such rationalizations was Lorna. She absolutely refused to see how repressing her anger could be anything but healthy.

"You just have to admit, Lorna," (by this point in the conversation I was quite upset) "that Ned knows when you are angry."

"No, I'm quite sure he doesn't."

"Come on! Ned has been living with you for over three years now. Do you mean to tell me he doesn't know when you are hiding your emotions from him?"

"Yes! I mean just that. You see, as soon as I get mad I go take a long walk. By the time I'm back I'm pretty mellow."

"Don't you think he knows why you need those long walks?"

"No. But even if he did, what can I do, scream at him?"

"You don't have to scream at Ned. You can let him know how angry you are without screaming."

"You've never seen me when I'm mad. I scream and holler and throw things. I lose all control."

"That's not because you let your anger out. That's because you keep it in. You let things build until your cork pops and you can't control yourself any more."

"I hope you don't think that screaming is going to help us get along better!"

"Now look, Lorna, I'm not saying screaming is going to help your relationship, and you know it. I'm saying that if you would only let Ned know you're angry as soon as you get angry, you would help your relationship."

"I don't see how getting mad is going to help any relationship."

There was no way to get through to Lorna. I tried several times, but she refused even to consider what I was saying to her. I never blamed her, however. I cannot blame anyone for thinking anger is something purely evil. We live in a social atmosphere that is tense about every angry display. Persons who "lose their temper" are regarded with disdain. With such constant conditioning, it does not surprise me that so many persons think of anger in wholly negative terms.

I'm Not Shouting

Some people fear anger because of their childhood experiences. Many of them lived with parents who did a lot of shouting and screaming at one another. The anxiety and frustration of living in a family where fighting was the norm can be enough reason to avoid every hint of unpleasantness. People from such families usually try to avoid more than anxiety and frustration, however. They are aware of the futility of fighting. After all of the shouting and name-calling had ended, their parents were no closer together, and the problem that caused the outburst was hardly touched.

Those who often witnessed their parents fighting think they know a lot about expressing anger. Yet, the people they watched shout and scream at each other knew very little about the genuine expression of feelings.

Often those who "boil over" are hiding from themselves and others the real source of their anger. They may be too proud or too afraid to admit what is really bothering them. For example, a young woman I met told me, "I used to get furious when Tom paid too much attention to other women, but I couldn't admit that. So I would let my anger build until I couldn't stand it any longer. Then I would start crying and screaming." No doubt the crying and screaming relieved some of her tensions, but it hardly touched the cause of her anger.

In such cases, crying, screaming, and throwing things are just other forms of repression. There is little difference between one person's shouting and another person's saying nothing. In both cases, the real cause of anger is repressed. Those who proudly boast, "I'm not afraid to let people know how I feel," are often just as repressed as those who hide from their anger by suffering in silence.

I remember trying to make this very point with Steve, a neighbor who was telling me how angry he got when he felt his wife was spending too much time with their children. "After a while I get jealous of my own kids," he confessed. "Then I get angry with Carly. Before you know it, I'm downright mean and hostile."

"Have you told Carly you get jealous of the children and wish she would spend more time with you?"

"Oh, she knows that."

"How does she know?"

"I'm not afraid to let her know when I'm mad. I really let go when I get angry."

"You may really let go, but do you tell Carly exactly why you are angry?"

"Not in so many words."

"Then how is she supposed to know what's bothering you?"

"Well, it's obvious."

"To you, maybe, but I don't see how it could be obvious to Carly."

"Yeah, I guess you're right. But don't you think she can figure out what's wrong? The same thing always gets me angry."

"Carly might think you are jealous of the kids, but she could also think of a lot of other things that might make you mad."

"I guess I'm actually scared to let Carly know what's bothering me. It sounds so stupid."

"I understand that. I know how embarrassing it is to admit what is making me angry."

"I just can't bring myself right now to admit to Carly that I'm jealous of our own kids."

"I know how you feel. I just hope you can quit pretending that Carly knows exactly what is bothering you. It takes a lot more than an outburst to express your anger."

Steve is hardly unique. Most of us have a difficult time showing our anger. Most of us also have trouble admitting that difficulty. But for some reason or other, those who hide their anger behind emotional outbursts pride themselves on expressing their feelings. Nothing could be further from the truth than that they are expressing their true feelings.

Don't Blame Me

Another way many of us defend ourselves from expressing our true anger is by blaming someone else. Such phrases as, "You make me mad," and "I can't stand you," place the blame for our upset on other people. As long as we are shouting accusations at others, we are unable to see just what causes our anger. Naturally, it is common for us, in the heat of an outburst, to blame someone else for our anger. It may not be fair to throw accusations at another person, but it certainly is human.

In calmer moments, either after the angry outburst has subsided or when we are not so volatile, we know that no one else *caused* our turmoil. We might have reacted to something another person did. Very rarely, however, does anyone deliberately provoke our anger. So that expressions like, "You make me mad," are not only unfair, they are inaccurate.

Once we realize others are not the cause of our anger and are determined not to blame them, we are faced with a problem. On the one hand, we would like to avoid accusing others. On the other hand, we do not want to remain silent. Something someone did has provoked us to anger and we want to say something. Yet there seems to be no choice except blame or silence.

There is an alternative, however. We can turn almost any unfair accusation into an honest statement. Instead of, "You make me angry," we can say, "I get angry when you do that." It may seem that there is only a semantic difference between the two statements. But far more than semantics is involved. When we say, "I get upset by your actions," we are not blaming, we are not accusing, we are not demanding change. At the same time, we are letting the other person know how we feel and what behavior brings out those feelings.

To fight fair in a relationship, we must learn to express our feelings. Then we are offering a gift of ourselves. We are letting someone share the intimate emotional life we usually keep hidden. Just as we let our lover know about the things that bring us peace, cause us joy, and create good moods, we need to let that lover also know about the things that provoke us to anger, distrust, and depression. It is all part of sharing ourselves with our lover.

Gina, a close friend, faced this very problem when her lover began to use hard drugs. She was very upset when she said, "Now every time Nick even smokes a joint I get angry."

"Why so mad?"

"I honestly think he is on the way to becoming an addict."

"Are you sure?"

"I'm not sure, really. More than anything else, I'm worried about him."

"I can understand that. Have you talked to Nick about your fears?"

"No."

"Don't you think he deserves to know what is making you angry?"

"Yes, but I don't know what to say to him."

"Why not?"

"I just don't think I have the right to tell him to stop using drugs."

"I agree."

"I mean, I don't know if Nick is too heavy into drugs. Even if he is becoming an addict, I have no right to tell him what he should do with his life."

"I couldn't agree with you more."

"Really? I guess I don't understand what you're saying to me, then."

"I think there is a big gap between telling someone to stop using drugs and complete silence."

"Like what?"

"Like telling Nick his use of drugs bothers you. You don't have to tell him to quit drugs in order to let Nick know that you are concerned for him."

"What's the difference? I would still be putting pressure on him."

"There's a lot of difference between those two statements. The first is a command, and the second is an expression of your self."

"Suppose Nick stops using drugs just because he doesn't want me to worry."

"That's his choice. And it's a long way from telling him to quit drugs."

None of us ever acts in complete freedom. Our choices are always colored by the people around us, the books we are reading, our physical environment. Even the weather has its own effect. To let another person know how and why we are angry, depressed, joyful, or subdued is going to affect that other person's behavior. It is to be hoped that by knowing our honest reactions, others will be better able to make their own decisions. Making a choice in view of how that choice will affect others is a far cry from being told what to do. When Nick finally chose to stop using hard drugs, he was affected by Gina's reactions. He was not trapped by her commands.

Tell Me When You're Mad

Fighting fair means more than just eliminating blame. We must also be sensitive to just how angry we can become. Often we let some small irritation grow out of proportion before we release our anger. The easiest way to increase personal turmoil is to hide from our anger. The longer we let it go unexpressed, the more it grows out of proportion to its cause.

Most of us think we are being sensitive to a lover's concerns when we conceal our anger. So we try to turn our mind elsewhere and forget about the irritations that cause us to be upset. There is no way to turn off emotion, however, and our anger usually grows until we can no longer contain it. Then when we express our feelings a real turmoil emerges.

The only honest way to express our feelings is to let our partner know what is bothering us just as soon as we experience it. At the instant we feel anger, we are in some position to keep it proportionate to its cause.

The other reason for expressing anger when it occurs is to help our partner know just what is bothering us. There are times when we think we have expressed our turmoil. But our description of the irritation often leaves our partner confused. Only when we say, "That's what bothers me. You're doing it right now, and I get mad every time you do it," can we be sure we have communicated the cause of our anger.

I had a talk with a student about just such a problem a number of years ago. Vicky had been living with Tim for nearly three years and they were quite happy together. Their problem centered around Tim's unconscious attempts to protect Vicky and treat her as helpless. This was particularly difficult for Vicky because she was extremely independent and deeply resented Tim's protective manner.

"Why don't you tell Tim he makes you angry when he treats you like a little girl?" I asked her.

"I've tried. It always seems to come out wrong, though. By the time I do talk to Tim I'm pretty upset and I say all kinds of things I don't mean."

"Sounds as if you wait until you have gotten really angry before you say anything."

"That's because I don't want to hurt his feelings. I know he only acts that way because he loves me. It's not his fault."

"Don't you think it would make more sense to talk to Tim about your anger before it gets so far out of hand? Then maybe you wouldn't be so likely to hurt him."

"Yes, but that's not the only problem."

"Really?"

"My other problem is trying to tell Tim exactly what's bothering me. I can never seem to pinpoint it for him."

"You've tried?"

"Many times. I tell him I don't want to be treated like a kid, but he always thinks in terms of letting me do the things I want to do, have my own friends, and stuff like that."

"But you're talking about something different from that, right?"

"Yes, It's more Tim's tone of voice, the unconscious things he expresses, the attitudes he has. Those things are hard to describe, but they are my biggest problem."

"Maybe you had better tell Tim about those things just as he is doing them. That way there can be no mistake."

"Oh, that's awfully hard."

"You bet it is, but I don't see any other way. You can't expect Tim to change his behavior when he isn't sure what annoys you."

It took Vicky several weeks to get up the courage to let Tim know when he was bothering her. She caught him one day insisting she stay in bed because of a virus she was fighting. She said, "That's the kind of thing that gets to me, Tim. If I want to risk getting more flu, that's my problem. Don't tell me what I can and can't do."

Tim was astounded. He had no idea that was the sort of thing that bothered Vicky. So it took him a long time to begin changing his attitudes. They were part of his personality and background. But he made a beginning. Vicky was then able to give him help and understanding. The source of the anger was expressed, and they were able to work together on dealing with its effects.

Watch Your Step

The fear of anger has another side. Besides being frightened for our relationship, most of us fear anger because it makes us vulnerable. Any time we say, "I'm getting angry at you," we are also laying ourselves open to the charge, "You've been getting on my nerves, too!" Most of us would just as soon not hear about our flaws. It seems better to avoid anger altogether.

Our great fear of being vulnerable is unfortunate. Only when we are vulnerable to one another can we draw close as human beings. The need for closeness in the unmarried relationship is often best satisfied after the partners have expressed their anger. The moments that follow are intensely personal. Our barriers are torn away and we see one another in our human frailties.

There is always the danger of losing a partner because of an angry outburst. That can happen. Yet those who express their anger and still remain open to one another usually strengthen their relationship. Expressed anger clears away hidden defenses, and the vulnerability that follows brings two persons closer together.

When one young woman talked about her happy relationship, my class imagined almost everything but anger as the source of her happiness. One woman immediately asked, "Did you have a happy childhood?"

"No," Maggie answered reflectively, "my parents separated when I was quite young. I was shifted from relative to relative most of my early life."

"Your husband, then," the same student said quickly. "He must be pretty well integrated."

"Of course, I think so," laughed Maggie, "but he doesn't seem to feel that way about himself."

A lot of other questions and answers left the class even more bewildered. Finally, in a kind of desperation, a young fellow asked, "What do *you* think makes your relationship work?"

Maggie was uneasy with the question. Finally she replied, "A lot of things. Most of the things that make it good would be beyond description. But one of the things that accounts for our happiness is our fights."

"Fights?" a lot of people repeated in a half-joking fashion.

"Yes, fights. We promised each other we would never go to bed angry. Sometimes that means staying up until one or two in morning fighting. We just fight and fight until we get everything out in the open. Then we go to bed in each other's arms."

The class did not want to hear that fights helped make Maggie's relationship with her lover happy. Like a lot of us, they wanted to hear of the idyllic moments, shared experiences, or planned activities. We are all looking for some easy formula that will bring us closer to our lovers. None of us wants to think that fighting has to be a part of the program. We spend too much time suppressing the angry word and hiding from the difficult encounter. Making anger integral to a good relationship would mean that our efforts to suppress it are damaging to our relationship. We would rather not hear that. Yet, it's true. Those who are happiest in their relationship are skilled at expressing anger. They know that some of the most poignant moments occur only after the angry word is spoken.

I Love You 9

Love is probably the most potent word in the English language. When it expresses a feeling that comes from deep within us, it implies a commitment. Each of us sees that commitment in a slightly different light, but few would deny that a serious commitment is implied by the word "love." In some fundamental way we seal a bond with the person to whom we express our love. Once we say, "I love you," our relationship with that other person changes. A commitment has been established.

Any time we love someone, we are vulnerable to that person. A lover's words and actions have great power to hurt us. Only after we express our feelings, however, does our lover experience that power. The lover who knows our vulnerability has a weapon. That the weapon may never be used does not change its potential.

It is not surprising that we want to escape from the word "love." It has serious consequences. Much better, it seems, to use the word casually and try to deny its meaning or, better yet, avoid saying it altogether. Then we seem to escape the consequences that are so frightening—the vulnerability and the commitment.

Naturally, there is no way to escape the consequences of using the word "love." When we avoid the commitment and vulnerability it demands, we also avoid the intimacy and sense of belonging that come with the proper expression of love. Many times I have heard someone say, "Oh, you don't have to say, 'I love you.' People can tell how you feel without spelling it out." I suppose the point could be argued. I can only say that whenever I have expressed my love for someone or heard another person express love for me, I was deeply affected. And I am not talking on a purely emotional plane. I mean that once the word "love" is used to express a deep feeling, I am changed by that experience.

I remember when June, a former student of mine, discovered this truth for herself. The experience was so unsettling that it not only affected her relationship with Greg, it affected her entire life. I remember she was still stunned when she told me, "I never thought expressing love was so important."

"I recall you made that point when you were in class last year."

"I was pretty certain of my position. I guess that was because I never heard anyone in my family express love directly. I knew my parents and brothers loved me. I just never could see why it was important to use the words."

"If you had never experienced the impact of the words, you couldn't be expected to know their importance."

"Exactly. Greg came from the same kind of background, so we just fell into a pattern of not expressing our love. We both knew it went deep, but somehow the words came hard. So for the first six months we lived together, neither of us ever used the word 'love.' "

"That's incredible."

"I suppose it sounds that way, but we were anxious to avoid throwing the word around. So many people abuse the word 'love,' and we were determined not to fall into that trap."

"So what happened?"

"Everything went on as usual until last month. It was one of those nights. The mood was right. The time was right. Everything seemed to be super-mellow."

"I know the kind of atmosphere you're talking about."

"Well, Greg couldn't contain himself. He said, 'June, I know we've avoided the word "love." And I guess that's all right. But tonight I want to tell you how much I love you. I want you to know I love you more than I have ever loved anyone. In fact, I am so in love with you it sometimes frightens me.' "

"Wow! That must have been some experience for you."

"I can't explain the impact. I have never been so affected by anything. It is as if I became new. Every part of me was affected. Nothing has been the same since that night."

"So the words did make a difference."

"I can't tell you how much. And in a way I was right. Nothing in our situation has changed, really. I already knew how much Greg cared about me. I knew it from his expression, his tone of voice, the little considerate things he did for me. But just hearing those words has changed my life."

June went on to tell me just how much her life was changed. After hearing Greg express his love, she had to tell him about her love for him. This was another experience that had deep-seated implications. From there it wasn't very long before June was expressing her feelings for others—her parents, her friends, her brothers. Each time, a new relationship was formed. As she said later, "An entirely new world opened up for me."

The Fear of Being Loved

Part of the reason most of us find it so difficult to express our love is our fear of being loved. When a parent, a brother, a sister, or a lover says, "I love you," the words can be embarrassing to us. Our mind can want to race past the tension they create. We may want to respond, but everything we might say seems awkward or conceited. No matter how we would like to reply when someone expresses affection for us, we usually end up ignoring the expression or saying something we later regret.

Again, we are divided within our self. Part of us longs to hear others express affection for us. We can even be angry over the lack of appreciation we usually experience. In our mind we often feel neglected and wish others paid more attention to us. Yet, another part of our personality cringes when someone uses the very words we long to hear.

Our internal reactions suggest we actually fear being loved. That possibility seems so preposterous that some people laugh at the thought. Yet, when we look at our reaction to affection, we can see our fear. Our need to turn praise into a joke, to skip past words of tenderness, to question even the most sincere expression of affection all indicate that we do, at some fundamental level, fear being loved. We may never understand that fear. We may never accept it. But we cannot deny its existence.

Maybe the fear of love is important to me because I had so much personal trouble with it. During my college days I was striving hard to gain the attention of others. I did most of this through my studies. I felt that I could attract attention by becoming proficient intellectually. I was completely unaware that I was effectively placing distance between myself and others by striving to attract such attention. Yet my fear would not permit me to call attention to myself directly.

The ironic thing about my pursuit of intellectual competence was my inability to accept praise even for my accomplishments. I would work hard for some goal or prize. Sometimes I spent long hours achieving recognition. But as soon as anyone would say, for example, "That was really good. You have a right to be proud," I would pass off the honor by saying something foolish like, "It really isn't very important." As soon as I had won the honor I hoped would bring me recognition, I rejected it as unimportant!

I am certain I was terrified of the very affection I craved. I was so frightened that I had to seek the esteem of others through my accomplishments, rather than looking openly for love. I was blind to the obvious paradox of my actions, however. I did not realize I was desiring and fearing the same thing simultaneously.

I can now look back and understand my conflict. I realize that two forces were at work within me. One side of my personality wanted love and affection. The other side was terrified that someone would actually give them to me. Those two sides still exist within me. There are still times when I fear hearing people tell me that I am important to them. There are also times when I can be upset because others do not appear to value me. I expect those two parts of me always to exist side by side.

The difference between the me-now and the me-then is important. I have learned to accept the two different persons I can be at times. I have come to believe it is all right to be searching for affection one day and fearful of its effects on another day. I now realize it isn't possible always to be consistent, to have logical feelings, or to do things that are reasonable. I can now be so unreasonable, inconsistent, and illogical as to fear being loved. And since it is now all right to fear being loved, I experience a lot less panic over being myself. More often I can be receptive to the affection others offer me.

The most important step in learning to be loved is to accept the fear that accompanies the expression of love. When we try to figure out why we are afraid, to ignore our fear, or to pretend we have no fear, we only distract ourselves. The trick is to quit nagging ourselves for being the way we are. If we can just let ourselves be fearful when that happens, we will be able to notice the signs of affection when they are offered.

I'm Not Worth It

The fear of being loved often arises out of feelings of worthlessness. Most of us, at one time or another, have experienced ourselves as unworthy of anyone's love. Those feelings for some persons are specific. For example, their parents may have told them they were worthless. Others have only a vague idea where their feeling of inadequacy came from. Whether the origin is clear or not, there is rarely any confusion about one's sense of worthlessness. Sometimes it is so strong that one can say, "I know that no one else could love me, because I don't even love myself."

Ironically, expressions of love are the only answer to the feelings of being worthless. When someone we love and trust expresses affection for us, we can see ourselves in new ways. We might try to rationalize by thinking, "She doesn't really know me or she could never say that." But however we try to explain away the impact, we are changed when we hear the words, "I love you," from someone who cares deeply for us.

This is one of the paradoxes of love. The only way to rise above our feelings of worthlessness is to hear expressions of love. Yet our inadequacy leads us to ignore and even avoid those expressions at times. It would seem there is no solution to the dilemma.

The paradox is most cruel to those who are caught in its immediate pull. With a bit of risk, we are able to hear the words, "I love you," from those we love. Maybe at first we can permit only a little of the impact to penetrate the barrier we put between ourselves and others. Normally, the experience is so satisfying that we cannot resist its pull for long. Sooner or later, we need to hear again that we have value in someone else's eyes. The movement may be slow, but it does happen. The day finally comes when we can look back and say, "I remember when I didn't even like myself. Now, thank God, I'm pretty good friends with me."

I discovered how much one young man's attitude toward himself had changed when I talked to him during a display of his photography. I was struck by the improvement in Floyd's technique, and told him, "You've really made progress since I last saw your work."

"Thanks. I think I have, too."

"Has anything special happened to account for so much improvement?"

"A lot of things, I suppose. More than anything else, I think my work got better after I met Angie."

"Oh, I didn't know you had a relationship right now."

"Angie and I moved in together about six months ago."

"That's great."

"Better than you can imagine. My entire outlook has changed over these last six months."

"How's that?"

"Well, when I was in your class, I was pretty negative about myself."

"I didn't know that."

"Most people didn't, but it was true. I didn't think I was worth very much and I didn't think anything I did was worth much, either."

"Angie changed all that."

"Angie changed all that. She saw something

in me no one else ever saw. She was convinced I was worthwhile."

"And she convinced you that you were worthwhile."

"It took quite a bit of time, but she has helped *me* see that I might have some value."

"Sounds as if that might have been a long way to come in six months."

"You have no idea. I don't think anyone could possibly know how much I disliked myself. I was so embarrassed by my attitude that I never let others know how miserable I was."

"And now your attitude has changed so much it even shows in your photography."

"That's just one way it shows. My whole life has changed. My relationships with other people are better. My attitude toward school is more positive. Even my attitude toward my parents has improved."

Floyd heard the various ways Angie expressed her love. It took him a good deal of time to let those expressions of love penetrate his own sense of worthlessness. As he came to believe Angie really loved him, however, he began to see the entire world around him in a more positive light. His sense of personal value made him look on what he did as worthwhile. The feeling of worthlessness began to dissolve because someone cared for him.

Don't Hurt Me

Our fear of rejection also prevents us from expressing our love. Most of us have a deep-seated fear that our love will not be returned. Probably nothing could hurt us more deeply than to tell someone, "I really care about you,"—and be greeted by silence.

The fear of being rejected is often well-founded. I have known many people who drew close to someone and risked opening themselves, only to be rejected by the one they trusted so completely. There is no easy way to recover from such an experience. Some people never do overcome the effects of this kind of rejection.

Even those who have never experienced a serious rejection often have difficulty opening themselves to others. Their fear may have its roots in an insecure family life, or it may originate elsewhere. But the origin does not seem to determine the strength of the fear. Some of the most fearful people cannot account for their rigid attitudes.

The fear of rejection will always be around. Even those who have known a long and happy relationship can experience it. The most intimate relationship holds moments of fear and doubt. There will, of course, be times when no fear stands between lovers and their ability to say, "I love you." The danger is that we let the expressions of love become too commonplace, or—at the other extreme—let fear dominate our ability to express affection.

In all aspects of expressing love, I find young people more sophisticated than ever before. Even the very young have a great understanding of the fears love can bring, as well as an appreciation of the joy implicit in love relationships. Many junior-high-school and even grade-school students are more sensitive to some aspects of love than their parents were. A junior-high-school student who lived down the street from me was anxious to talk to me one day. "Do you have a few minutes?" she asked hesitantly.

"I sure do, Ginger. What's up?"

"It's about this boy at school."

"I guess I might have figured that out."

"Yeah. Well, it's serious."

"I'm sure it is."

"I mean, we're serious. We've been going together for about three months now. I really like Jack, and I think he really likes me."

"And?"

"And I want to tell him how much I like him."

"Why don't you?"

"I'm afraid he might not feel the same way."

"I see what you mean."

"You see, that happened to me once before. I was crazy about this boy who took me out a few times. When I told him how much I liked him, he dropped me completely. He never took me out again."

"And you're afraid that will happen again."

"I know that's crazy. I'd only gone out with the guy who dropped me about two or three times. Jack and I have been going together for about three months."

"But that doesn't change your fear."

"That's right. Even though I know it's different with Jack and me, I never quit being scared."

"You don't want to be hurt again."

"I just couldn't stand another rejection."

"Well, I'll tell you, Ginger. You always have a choice. You can tell Jack how much you like him or you don't have to. But there will never be any way for you to tell him you like him without taking a chance. There will always be a risk involved."

"That's what I thought."

Before the week was over, Ginger had told Jack how much she liked him. Jack was honestly surprised. He was crazy about Ginger, but never guessed she felt the same way about him. The two of them were so happy they could hardly stop talking. "I would have come to tell you a couple of days ago," Ginger said when she saw me, "but I didn't want to leave Jack."

A New World

Those who learn to express affection for one another open up a new world. Often no more than a few words of tenderness stand between a couple and a personal moment of sharing. With a little sensitivity to each other, love partners can release emotions that might otherwise remain unexpressed.

There will always be some fear around to justify a decision to let a warm emotion go unexpressed. We never completely escape the fear of rejection and our feelings of inadequacy. At the same time, the rewards implicit in expressing our feelings are overwhelming. Nothing can compare to the new world of emotional closeness that rewards those who dare to say, "I love you."

Cindy, a young woman who had been in one of my encounter groups, wrote me a letter in which she described her experience in growing close to her partner. *"When Andy and I first moved in together, we promised we would always be honest with each other. In the be-*

ginning, this meant saying a lot of unpleasant things. We had to let one another know the things that bugged us. There were even times when I thought we were on the verge of breaking up. Somehow I knew we had to keep it up if we were going to make it as a couple. But many times I just wanted to give up.

"Finally, the turmoil began to ease up a little. We had been open about our anger and had reached an honest level with each other. I thought, for a while, we were over the worst of our troubles. But even before we had begun to completely settle down, I was beginning to feel a pressure to express my affection. I wanted to let Andy know how much I cared for him, and how much I appreciated his willingness to work through so many angry feelings. That may not seem like much of a problem to you, but it sure was for me.

"You see, I've always had a hard time expressing my affection. My sister and I were brought up in a very strict religious atmosphere, where 'self-control' meant holding in all your emotions. I can't ever recall anyone saying, 'I love you.' I don't even remember my mom and dad using the words. So I was scared to death when it came to telling Andy how much I cared. I was so frightened he didn't love me the way I loved him. I just couldn't stand having him not reciprocate, once I had told him how much I cared. In many ways, this was an even more difficult period than our angry period. But we had learned a lot by expressing our anger. We learned how to have faith in one another, and also learned that things will eventually work out if you are really honest with one another.

"Things did work out. We learned to say, 'I love you.' Now when the moment is right, we both can rather spontaneously express our affection. There is nothing like it! An evening, a day, even a week can be changed by a word of tenderness. A grey day can suddenly become bright and clear. A moody day can become happy and fulfilling. It is as if there is a world hidden underneath our day-to-day routine. And when the moment is right you can uncover that world of love by just saying, 'I love you!' "

I've Got to Be Free

10

There are many reasons couples choose to live together instead of marrying. One of the most significant is their desire to keep their independence and freedom. They saw their parents and other couples trapped by the legal bond imposed by marriage. They want to avoid that trap. So they shun legal ties in hopes they will remain free of the psychological restrictions often created by marriage.

The sacrifices unmarried couples make in order to avoid marriage are often considerable. They can suffer severe criticism by their friends, families, and even society in general for living together. For most of them, it is worth incurring the scorn of others if they can maintain their freedom. It is ironic, then, that while maintaining their external freedom from marriage, many couples still sacrifice their personal freedom. They trap themselves inside their own emotions. The fear of what their lover might say effectively prevents them from expressing anger, love, boredom, or loneliness. They are so afraid of offending, hurting, or losing their partner that they literally cannot "be themselves."

True independence can only be achieved when partners are free to express themselves to each other. No external set of rules can guarantee that independence. I have known too many couples who try to be free by making sure the housework is shared, the expenses are shared, the care of the children is shared. While they divide everything equally, they do not express to one another the feelings that result. So often, then, the equal division of tasks that was supposed to free them only drives them further into their own feelings of restriction.

It is important for people living together to share the work as well as the play that makes their life happen. This attitude prevails in unmarried relationships, and is encouraging to see. At the same time, it is sad to observe couples who think that the sharing of tasks will free them psychologically. The only way two people can be free is through an internal willingness to experience themselves fully even while they live with someone else. The act of being ourselves, even though it hurts, frustrates, angers, or upsets our partners, is the freeing element in the relationship. Without such expression with our partners, we have little chance to establish a free relationship.

Sid always comes to mind when I think of someone who felt trapped by what was supposed to be an open relationship. He stayed down the hall from us while he was living with Ruth. Neither made any pretense about living together. Their door and mailbox prominently displayed different last names. Many of the people in our apartment building were disturbed by this arrangement, but Sid and Ruth were apparently untouched by criticism. They seemed to have a truly free relationship. At least it appeared that way until the day Sid said to me,

"Well, I have to go now. I have to scrub out the toilets."

"You have to scrub out the toilets?"

"I know. You're going to say that's no job for a man."

"No, I'm not. As a matter of fact, I usually do the toilets at our place. But it sounds as if you can't stand the job."

"I hate it. I hate it more than anything I can think of."

"Does Ruth know how you feel?"

"Oh, no. I don't dare tell Ruth about my attitudes. She would be terribly upset."

"I don't get it."

"Well, Ruth wants to make sure we have a completely open relationship. That means we have to share the housework evenly."

"What kind of open relationship is it if you can't tell Ruth how you feel?"

"I know. That's what I keep telling myself. But Ruth has definite ideas about just what couples who live together should do."

"It sounds as if the rules would be the same no matter who Ruth was living with."

"As a matter of fact, you're right. Ruth has lived with three guys, including me. The rules are always the same."

"I don't think I could stand following the same rules that applied to two people before me."

"It's getting to me, too. I don't know how much longer I can take it."

The relationship lasted only a couple of months longer. Sid finally left Ruth. He said to her, "I can't stand being just another guy. It's as if you can't see me." The fault was not entirely Ruth's, however. Until the last moment, Sid never expressed his feelings about being just one more man in Ruth's life. He was afraid to let her know how he felt about the many rules, and what they were doing to their relationship. Instead, he went along, with an occasional irrational explosion to relieve his tension, until he could stand it no longer. Then he left. He never saw himself as a prisoner to his fears. He was unaware of his stifled freedom. He and Ruth had talked too much about independence and freedom to realize that they were keeping one another dependent and captive.

I'll Lean on You

Most of us spend a good deal of time worrying about how others will react to feelings we keep hidden from them. We can free ourselves of this worry only by revealing these inner emotions. As long as we hide them, we maintain a dependent relationship with others. Repressing our anger, for example, might be caused by the fear that we might lose a friendship we depend on. Reluctance to admit boredom might be caused by the fear that others would take offense. Our fear of showing affection might be caused by doubts about what the other person would think. In each case, we are restricting an expression of feeling because of our dependence on the approval of others. If we were free of such dependence, we could let others know of our feelings as they emerged.

The times when we tell others of our boredom, our anger, or our affection are usually so rare that we seldom experience the great freedom such expression brings. Once we have overcome our fear and told someone of our anger, for example, there follows a great sense of relief. We feel good about our self. That good feeling contains a note of confidence, adequacy, and reassurance. We feel a deep sense of independence from the judgments of others, the reassurance that it is all right for us to be ourselves and to experience our own feelings.

It is not easy to stand out before others without masks or pretenses. Each time we do, however, we assert our independence. Our expression of feelings gives us an awareness of freedom. We have accepted our reactions as our own, and let others know how we experience ourselves.

This kind of independence is the essence of personal growth. Our ability to express ourselves is a way of saying, "This is who I am." To the extent that we can assert our independence, we will not be preoccupied with wondering how we appear to others. We need not worry about what will please others, impress them, or entertain them. We can increasingly depend on being ourselves. That is growth in the most fundamental sense of the word.

I did my funniest pretending when I was in high school. In those days I was involved with being popular. The important thing in the crowd I joined was popularity. Some created their popularity out of their athletic ability. Others shone brightly because of their intelligence. Still others were great conversationalists. I felt I knew how each person maintained an attraction for the group.

One day when I was considering the reasons for each person's popularity, I suddenly realized there was nothing that maintained my esteem in the group. I remember saying to myself, "I am the only person who is not outstanding at anything. There is no reason for my friends to continue to invite me to their homes and to their parties." I started to panic. The more I thought about the situation, the more I feared others would begin to leave me off the lists of those who were invited.

Once I calmed down, I decided I had better create a personality that others would find attractive. The next time the group was out together, I observed my friends carefully. In my mind the most attractive person was Frank. Further reflection led me to believe the thing that made Frank so attractive was his casual attitude. No matter what happened, Frank was calm, cool, and collected. The more I thought about it, the more I was convinced that I had better get busy on a similar casual image.

The parties after that were a chance for me to practice my casual approach. I made sure that my posture looked relaxed. I took time when I answered questions and joined in conversations. I even prided myself on being more casual than Frank. That was certain to be a plus for me when people compared us. The only problem was that my casual image was tearing me up inside. I was so worried about being casual, I was a nervous wreck. I started to hate going to parties. It was too much work trying to keep up my casual appearance. Besides, others did not seem to pay any more attention to the casual-me I worked so hard to create. In a rather short time, I gave it up as a bad experience.

I was not aware of it at the time, but my pretense had made me completely dependent on my friends. Even though they did not know it, I was changing my personality for them. I was becoming casual to impress them and prompt their friendship. There was no possibility of personal growth. I was too caught up in trying to be someone I was not and never could be. My own personality not only went undeveloped, it was distorted. I could not continue my personal growth until this period of pretense had ended.

You Asked for It

One reason we avoid self-expression is the fear of being responsible for our feelings. If we discover we are angry at a friend and express that anger, for example, we must take the consequences. We might be responsible for hurt feelings, for arousing anger in return, for a damaged friendship.

Most of us fear this kind of responsibility. We would rather not be in a position where anyone can point at us and say, "There is the one who caused it all." Our only defense might be to admit the irrationality of our feelings. We might protest, "I can't be held responsible for my emotions." Yet we know we can be and are. Much better, it seems, to hide our emotions from others. Then there will be no chance of hurting anyone, falling in love with the wrong person, losing our job, or causing our lover grief.

Jenny was terribly upset with the consequences of expressing her feelings. She was in my class at the time she came to me in distress over a fight she and Dale had had the night before. "I'm just miserable," she said, in a voice choked with tears.

"What happened?"

"I think Dale and I will be breaking up."

"Oh, that is bad."

"That's not the worst part. The worst part is that I'm responsible."

"You're responsible. Why are you responsible?"

"I was the one who started the whole thing. I told Dale I was angry with him for seeing other women."

"Well, did you feel that way?"

"Yes. But if I hadn't said anything, Dale would never have fought with me, and we might not be breaking up."

"Now, wait a minute. You're blaming yourself because you told Dale his relationships with other women were upsetting you?"

"That's right."

"I can understand your being upset because you are on the verge of splitting up. But I can't see how you can hold yourself responsible because you told Dale what was bothering you."

"Dale had every right to be himself."

"And it seems to me, you had every right to be yourself and let Dale know about your feelings."

"I had no right to be upset over what Dale was doing."

"That makes it sound as if you can control your feelings. Do you have some knob that turns your emotions on and off?"

"No, but—"

"Then it seems to me you had an obligation to let Dale know what reactions you were having to him."

"I don't think you understand the situation at all."

Jenny was too upset to hear what I was trying to say. On another occasion, we were able to communicate much better. The basic problem was one most of us share. We would rather not be held responsible for our feelings. Dale's other relationships were irritating Jenny. Sooner or later she had to say something. But when she did, she was unhappy with the results. Like a lot of us, she was frightened by the consequences of expressing her feelings.

Don't Leave Me

As we have noted, couples who live together have many reasons for failing to express their feelings. One of the most significant is the fear of losing a partner. Consequently, many unmarried couples fail to achieve personal independence because they cling too closely. As long as they are saying to one another, "I can't tell you how I really feel for fear you might not love me any longer," there is little hope they can grow in freedom.

Ironically, the fear of losing a partner also restricts the love possible between two persons. As long as we place restrictions on a lover, we will feel that the restrictions are helping to maintain the relationship. But it is only when we give complete freedom to our lover that we experience the heights to which our love can grow.

Often, we find ourselves caught between hopes and feelings. Our hope for our partner may be complete freedom, while our emotions can press us to cling. The question we are confronted with is, "How can I satisfy my desire to give my partner freedom without being dishonest about my jealous feelings?"

The conflict may never be resolved. Many couples who have lived together for years are still unable to cope with their desire to be free and, at the same time, their wish to restrict their partners. Yet there is an immediate solution to the desire to be honest about our feelings. We can say to our lover, "I want you to be free to be with others and, at the same time, I am uneasy about the very relationships I would like to encourage." Just because we are unhappy with our feelings does not mean we need to hide them.

Lois, a young student of mine, was having trouble with this conflict. "I just have to stop being so jealous over Rod's other friends," she told me anxiously.

"What's wrong with your jealousy?"

"Well, I think Rod should be free to be with anyone he wants to be with."

"I agree with you."

"Agree with me about what?"

"I too think Rod should be free to be with anyone he chooses. I just don't think it's necessary for you to get over your jealousy in order for him to do that."

"You think I should hide my jealousy?"

"No. As a matter of fact, I think it's important for you to express your jealousy. I believe Rod has every right to know how jealous you are and how much you want him exclusively."

"But that will tie him down. He won't be as

free, once he knows how I feel, to be with other people."

"That's possible. But how he reacts to your jealousy is his decision. If he decides to restrict himself in order to reduce your jealous feelings, he is free to do that."

"I'm not sure I understand."

"I want you to tell Rod about both sides of your feelings. I want you to tell him how much you would like to see him free and, at the same time, how much you would like to keep him all to yourself. His response to those feelings is his choice."

It took Lois some time before she could tell Rod just how she felt. By then she was living in another city. About a year later she wrote me, *"I finally took your advice and told Rod about my jealousy. At first he was upset by what I was saying. He thought I was telling him he wasn't supposed to see other people as much. His first reaction was to cut back on his social life. I began to hate myself for saying anything, and my desire to stamp out my jealousy became even greater.*

"After about a month, we finally talked about my feelings long enough that I could get through to him. This time he understood. We had a long talk, and he finally heard me say, 'But even though I'm jealous, I want you to be free to form other relationships.' After that talk, he picked up where he had left off with others. I was happy he was back doing what he wanted to do, but I was also bothered by the amount of time he wanted to be away.

"After spending some more time feeling

*sorry for myself while Rod was with other peo-
ple, I decided to form other relationships myself.
I found myself really growing and becoming
much happier. In fact, I think Rod became a bit
jealous of my time away from him! In any event,
my attitudes began to change. I realized the time
Rod does spend with me he freely chooses. Even
though he has a lot of other friendships, I'm still
by far the most important person for him. So I
guess the story has a happy ending after all."*

A Paradox

Paradoxically, our fondest hope for our lover
can be a subtle form of bondage. We might want
our partner to be more sensitive, more understanding, less unkempt, or less troubled. Our
motives can be selfish or even, at times, nearly
altruistic. Our desire that our partner be more
sensitive, for example, might not be for our own
sake. Our hope may be that our lover become as
sensitive with others as he or she is with us.

As long as our desires take the form of expectations, however, they place a burden on our
partner. As we all know, there is no way of
simply deciding to become more sensitive, more
loving, or less selfish. Such qualities do not develop by determined effort alone. There is even
less chance of becoming different in our attitudes when we are near someone who expects
that change.

Even when we know our expectations exert
pressure, however, we cannot will them away. It
is no easier for us to expect less of our lover than
it is for our lover to become instantly sensitive or
understanding. What we can and must do, however, is express the paradox as we experience it.

We can say, "I want so much for you to fulfill all of your potential. At the same time, I want you to be yourself. I know you can't do both of those things at the same time, and I don't expect you to. But I want you to know I have both of these hopes for you."

In the end, we cannot escape the paradox. We must try to accept our lover just as he or she is. Without that acceptance, our partner can never have the inner ease even to think of growth. At the same time, we need to express our expectations. Unless we do, we are hiding from the truth. Even more important, our expectations encourage our lover to recognize, and eventually fulfill, every bit of potential. It is difficult to live with paradox, but such paradoxes contain much of the truth about life and love.

Elinor was seriously upset by her desire for her lover's freedom and her simultaneous expectations for him. "I just can't see why Chuck doesn't stand up to his mother," she told me a bit frantically.

"In what way?"

"She still treats him like a little boy! In her eyes, he has never grown up."

"And you don't understand his reaction to her attitude?"

"I want him to let her know he is a grown man and has his own life to lead."

"I realize that you have your hopes for him, but tell me, haven't you ever been in Chuck's position?"

"Oh, sure! My parents used to treat me as if I was still a child, too. But I finally told them I was fully grown and had to be free to live my own life."

"That wasn't easy, was it? I mean, it surely took you a long time to get up enough courage to say that."

"It certainly did."

"Don't you think Chuck deserves the same freedom to wait until he's ready to confront his mother?"

"Oh—I never thought of it like that. Of course you're right. I just get impatient, that's all."

"It's all right to be impatient. I even want you to let Chuck know when you are impatient. But I also think you should give him freedom to wait until he's ready to confront his mother."

"You don't want much, do you? How can I tell him I'm impatient and still let him feel free to wait?"

"I wish I knew. I guess it is impossible to wish hard someone would change and still let him know you want him to be himself. We can only try."

This is one more paradox of the love relationship. We want to be free and, at the same time, to restrict our lover. There is no resolution to this paradox. We can only accept it as integral to our love. Ironically, in our ability to accept this conflict in our feelings, we also discover new depths to our love.

It's Time to Split II

Couples who live together may decide to end their relationship for any number of reasons. Some find they are attracted to different parts of the country. Others realize they will not be able to solve their financial difficulties. Still others give in to parental pressure. A great number of couples simply discover they are incompatible. The reasons for separating are probably as varied as the couples who decide to separate.

Unfortunately, separation in the minds of most people is strongly linked to a failure—so much so that many couples who end their relationship for the best possible reasons are convinced they have failed.

I hope I am not leaving the impression I think separation is an easy matter to manage. It is not. For couples who care about one another, the separation process is filled with emotion—most of it difficult to handle. Rather, I am saying that most partners who separate are too willing to judge themselves failures. Maybe they did fail in their relationship. Many do. But those who automatically equate separation with failure can do a great disservice to themselves and their partners.

Harriet illustrated the distortion which can be created by a sense of failure. She kept telling me over and over again how she and George had failed. "I've thought about it and thought about it. I just can't figure our where we went wrong."

"What makes you so sure you did something wrong?"

"We split, didn't we?"

"Yes, you did. But I know a lot of couples who split up that I don't consider failures."

"What are you talking about?"

"For the past thirty minutes you have been telling me how you and George have failed. Yet every time I try to find out how you consider yourselves failures, you draw a blank."

"I really *don't* know where we went wrong."

"And I'm saying that maybe your separation was no one's fault."

"But we loved each other so much."

"Who says that love is enough to keep a relationship together. I know a lot of couples who love each other but are simply incompatible."

"Surely someone is to blame for their incompatibility."

"Look, that's why I used the word 'incompatible.' That word, in my mind at least, doesn't place blame. Some people separate even though there is no one to blame."

"Well, then, who is to blame for their incompatibility?"

"Boy, this is really hard. Incompatibility

means you want to live in California and George wants to live in New York. Incompatibility means you want a large family and George can't stand children. Incompatibility means . . ."

"Are you trying to tell me that two people can love each other and not be able to stay together?"

"It's not easy, but I'm trying."

I found out later there was good reason for Harriet's obtuseness. What I was trying to tell her grated against everything she believed about love. She was raised in a home dominated by strict religious principles. Harriet's mother was divorced early and had never remarried. She spent the rest of her life blaming Harriet's father for the failure of their marriage.

When Harriet decided to live with George, it was her first step away from home. Naturally, Harriet's mother was in turmoil over a relationship she believed would send her daughter straight to hell. Harriet took a big step when she defied her mother and moved in with George. She had not yet settled down when she and George decided to separate. No wonder she could not hear me when I told her there need be no blame attached to a separation.

Be Prepared for the Worst

The fear of failure is enough to pressure most couples into avoiding any thoughts of separation. This is unfortunate. Couples who hide from the possibility of separation distort the true test their relationship might be. They cannot easily admit the inconsistencies, the irritations, and the grievances that weaken their stability.

Those who are sensitive to separation as a possibility are less likely to hide from their weaknesses. They are more apt to say to their partner, for example, "I guess you noticed my moodiness," and talk through such difficulties. They know that by trying to hide their own troubling behavior they are increasing the risk of separating. They know the best way to make separation distant is by expressing their weaknesses so that their partner will better understand them and their moods.

Those of us who remain aware of the possibility of separating are also more likely to be sensitive to our partner's feelings. When we know that the quality of our relationship is what ultimately keeps us together, we tend to be aware of our partner's needs. We are more likely to compliment, to admire, to express appreciation. Those who think of their relationship as a fragile thing will be alert for ways to strengthen it.

This realistic attitude also helps those who finally do separate. The couples who have not considered separation find parting extremely difficult. The pain can last for years and, in some cases, actually precipitate serious emotional turmoil. Those with more realistic attitudes are saved unnecessary pain. There is no way to eliminate the pain of separation entirely. We can, however, put it in a realistic context.

More than any other person, Paula impressed me with her attitude toward the fragile nature of her relationship with Rudy. She was probably more sensitive than most because, as she said, "I've lost a lot during my lifetime."

"Lost what?"

"To begin with, I lost my parents when I was five. I had to live with my grandparents after that."

"I see what you mean."

"You've only heard the beginning. My grand-parents died before I was eight, and after that I was raised in an orphanage."

"That must have been hard."

"It was. It probably accounts for the failure of my first marriage."

"My gosh! You lost your husband, too."

"I told you. I've lost a lot over the years."

"You certainly have."

"But I'm not surprised I lost my first husband."

"Why is that?"

"I can look back now and see how each loss made me cling just a little bit harder. When I lost my dad, I clung harder to my mom. When I lost my mom, I clung harder to my grandparents. By the time I got married, I was clinging just as hard as I could."

"I can see that."

"My husband couldn't take it. He just felt stifled. I can't blame him, though. I was fearful most of the time. I was afraid he would be killed, or he would fall in love with someone else, or he would lose interest in me. It must have been awful for him."

"But you don't have that kind of relationship with the guy you're living with now."

"With Rudy? Oh, no. Rudy has been fantastic. He has taught me the value of risking. He has helped me see how important it is to face the possible end of our relationship."

"That's great!"

"It sure is. Every morning now when I get up, I say to myself, 'Today I have to risk my entire relationship with Rudy'."

"You really do that? You consciously open yourself to the end of your relationship?"

"Yes, I do. It's the only way I know to avoid that deceptive clinging I almost instinctively do. If I think of the risk instead, I am more apt to be a partner to Rudy and less likely to try to control him."

Few of us think in terms of the extremes, as Paula did. We have not faced the insecurities that she did at such an early age. The principle is the same for us, however. If we do not think in terms of risking our relationship, we will also cling and be possessive. By risking everything, we can open ourselves and our partners to much richer rewards.

Don't Leave Me

Probably the deepest pain suffered by separating couples is the sense of loss. No matter how important it might be for them to separate, those who have become involved with one another will experience it. And the pain of loss is something we all dread. Most of us have experienced too much of it over the years. It is there whenever two close friends separate. Whether we are a child leaving the neighborhood, a high-school graduate leaving for college, or a lover saying goodbye to a partner, pain is around to make life depressing.

What most of us are not aware of is our tendency to cover this pain with anger. Just as we start to experience the pain of loss, we can find our partner irritating us more than at any time in the past. We so easily become aggravated and begin thinking, "I'll be glad when you're gone." It is easier to be angry than it is to experience our loss. As long as we are in a state of outrage, we can block out the deep-seated pain that cannot be controlled.

The cowardly way to separate is to leave with unexpressed bitterness toward our partner. Then all the memories of our relationship can be blocked out by our lingering anger. No wonder so many couples separate on this note of anger. That seems to be the only way to escape from pain. Only the most courageous couples can sit down and talk through their differences before they separate.

Couples who can do this will still experience the pain of loss. Under the circumstances, talking it out may seem to be some form of self-punishment. That is not the case. Such talks reflect a mature attitude. Only those who can look carefully at their separation and its causes will be able to grow from their experiences. They will see more clearly their own weaknesses and strengths, and they will understand themselves better before they enter another relationship. With this understanding, they will have a much better chance of succeeding the next time.

Leo almost instinctively knew what I was talking about the day I mentioned the pain of separation in class. Afterwards, we talked about his separation from Joan, and it was a nearly classic case. "As the time grew near for us to separate," he said, "I became more and more upset with Joan."

"Did your upset center on anything specific?"

"Not really. I was mostly annoyed with the way she would repeat things I said, the way she would expect me to know when she was upset, or the way she pulled on her fingers when she was nervous."

"I assume she had done these things before."

"Oh, sure. We had talked about all of them.

But once we set a date to separate, I stopped talking about how they irritated me. It was almost as if I wanted to be angry with her."

"You wanted to be angry with her?"

"Yeah. Then I could say to myself, 'I'm really glad Joan's not around any more. She used to drive me crazy.' "

"I understand that feeling."

"The problem was that the anger was getting all out of proportion. I was beginning to hate Joan and blame her for all the trouble we had."

"So what did you do?"

"I finally sat down and told Joan about my feelings and how they were becoming unreasonable. I told her I didn't want that, and thought it was unfair of me."

"How did she respond?"

"You'll never believe this. She was going through the same thing. She was becoming bitter toward me for ruining everything."

"So what happened?"

"We sat down and had a long talk. We talked about all the strengths and failures of our relationship. We might say we exchanged notes. And you know what happened?"

"No."

"I suddenly felt as if I didn't want to leave Joan any more."

"Seriously? You mean you might want to stay together?"

"Oh, no. We never will make it living together. No, I just mean that I think I saw Joan for the first time before we separated."

"That must have been something."

"It was. Now I miss her a lot. And if we hadn't had that last talk, I might never have missed her at all. She would just be the hostile gal I used to live with."

Not many people can be so honest when they are on the verge of separation. Most would rather follow Leo's early course and remember all the difficulties so that they could place blame. But Leo and Joan did the courageous thing and looked carefully at each other just before they said goodbye. They had never been able to see one another so clearly. That only made parting more difficult, but they were both stronger people for having had the experience.

Where Does It Hurt?

When couples resort to anger to cover the pain of loss, they cover a great deal more than that. Beyond the central core of loss are many other doubts, fears, and misgivings. Separation causes some to fear being alone again, causes others to feel depressed, and causes still others to feel abandoned. In each case, we are talking about pain that is peculiar to certain persons. Unlike the pain of loss, these feelings are not shared by all who decide to end their relationship.

The importance of these special kinds of pain is the insight they give us into our own personality. Like fingerprints, they identify us in our unique reactions to the separation process. These fears, doubts, and misgivings give us a rare opportunity to look at our inner self. The stress of a separation will make us conscious of traits we might never come to recognize in ordinary circumstances.

We could, for example, find we are terribly afraid of the loneliness that might follow separation. When our fear of being alone clearly reaches uncommon proportions, we would do well to consider the meaning of our reactions. Is there, somewhere in the back of our mind, a fear of loneliness we had not realized was there? Do we react to other stressful situations with fear? Does an unconscious fear of being left alone drive us to cling to our partner? By giving us the chance to see our self a little more clearly, separation can reveal feelings we seldom recognize in ourselves.

Our discoveries will have even more impact if we share them with our partner. Maybe our partner is aware of a fear we never noticed. Our partner may even have felt us cling, and could describe the impact such clinging had on our relationship. The insights possible under stress can be significant. The temptation to hide from the turmoil caused by stress will be strong. If we can resist that temptation, however, separation can have its maturing effect.

When Terry told me about her separation from Al, she was aware of the insights such a period can bring. "At first, I was too embarrassed to admit I was depressed," she told me in a therapy session.

"Embarrassed?"

"Yes. You see, I don't recall ever being depressed before."

"Never? You were never depressed at any time in your life?"

"See! That's the kind of reaction I always got. It made me wonder."

"I'm not surprised."

"Then Al left me. I was so depressed I couldn't hide my sadness."

"How did you square that with your previous claim of a depression-free existence?"

"That's just it. I couldn't. My reactions made a liar out of me."

"So what did you do?"

"I tried to cover up my gloom. I tried to pretend I was happy and hoped my depression would lift."

"Did that work?"

"Not at all. I just got more and more down."

"I hope you finally got around to talking about it with Al."

"To make a long story short, I finally did tell Al what was happening."

"How did he react?"

"At first he was pretty defensive. But once he saw I wasn't blaming him, he was able to talk quite freely with me."

"What did he say?"

"He told me he was surprised every time I told someone I never had a bad mood. He thought I was lying to my friends. He said he saw me depressed a lot. He told me my normal expression seemed sad to him."

"That must have come as a surprise."

"It sure did. I really thought my life was free of sadness, and then my lover tells me he sees it all the time."

Terry and Al talked a great deal more about Terry's sadness before they separated. In fact, in the month before they parted, they talked more personally than they had ever talked before. Those last talks helped them remain friends. They now recognize their incompatibilities and have no illusions about becoming partners again. Rather, like all close friends, they share confidences and react personally to one another in ways that are nourishing for both of them.

Growing Up

An expression sometimes used by couples who have separated is, "I learned a lot during that relationship." Often it is accompanied by a great deal of bitterness. Whether or not there is bitterness, however, a fundamental truth is involved. Even in relationships that are difficult and filled with turmoil, couples generally learn from their experiences.

Often the learning that takes place in a relationship is enough to change a person substantially. It is even common for both partners to find themselves dramatically changed by their experiences. In the best situations, the two people grow in ways that bring them closer together. There are equally healthy relationships, however, which free couples to grow apart. This kind of relationship can help partners discover themselves, only to find their true self no longer wants to live with the person who made the discovery possible.

How can we talk of such a relationship as a failure? The process of discovery has done more than end a relationship. It has helped two people find themselves and, in most cases, achieve greater happiness. It seems much more appropriate for partners in such an experience to thank one another and remain friends. They have given one another the freedom to grow and to express their own individual uniqueness. There may be no greater gift.

The relationship that opened me to the possibilities of the good separation was shared by two of my former students. They had lived together and parted before Dorothy told me one day after class, "I never would have been able to take this class in the evening if it weren't for Perry."

"How is that?"

"Perry is taking care of the kids so I can attend."

"That's really nice, but I'm surprised."

"Why are you surprised?"

"As I remember your relationship with Perry, you two were always fighting."

"You have a good memory. But that was while we were together. Now we're pretty good friends."

"Really? In what way?"

"In just about every way. Besides taking care of the kids, Perry still goes out with me. Every now and then we will go dancing. Sometimes we take in a movie. Occasionally Perry will just come over so we can play with the kids and talk."

"It sounds as if you two are better friends now than when you were living together."

"Oh, we definitely are. When we lived together we were constantly at each other's throats."

"I remember."

"I think we both grew up during our fights and squabbles. We were like little kids who had to get a lot of anger out of our systems. I will always be grateful to Perry for letting me do that, and I think he feels the same way toward me."

"Any chance you will ever get back together again?"

"Never! After I got myself all fought out, I

realized it was my anger that bound me to Perry. Once the anger was released, he had no more fascination for me. Sounds crazy, doesn't it?"

"Not really."

"Anyway, I will never be able to think of not having Perry for a friend, but I don't think I could ever see him again as a lover."

Dorothy and Perry grew up in their relationship. Part of their mutual attraction was their ability to vent their anger on one another. They both needed to do that desperately. No wonder they are grateful to each other. Few people will allow others to express such strong emotions. Their ability to release their anger matured both of them. In their case, separation did not signal failure, but rather success.

Let's Stick Together
12

Many people assume that living together necessarily implies a temporary arrangement. This attitude may be understandable among those who have never had the experience of living together. It is disconcerting, however, to find couples living together who assume their relationship must be temporary.

Possibly unmarried couples are being affected by the attitudes of society around them. There is a clear prejudice in society against couples who live together without being married. In any event, unmarried couples reveal their own prejudice against living together permanently when they say, for example, "After we've been together for a while, we will probably get married," or, "I'm not sure when we will get married." Such phrases are troubling because they identify permanence only with marriage. It is as if they are saying, "If it turns out that we have a good relationship, we will have to get married." They refuse to think of alternatives.

There is no intrinsic contradiction in a permanent unmarried relationship. In fact, for some couples the unmarried relationship has a much better chance to achieve permanence than does marriage. We need not attack marriage to come to this conclusion, either. Marriage will always be the right relationship for some. But it is vital that all couples become aware that they have a choice.

A prejudice in favor of marriage had affected Charlotte in her relation with Hal. They had been living together for about three years and were thinking seriously of marriage. "I guess we are going to have to face up to it," she told me gloomily.

"Face up to what?"

"Marriage."

"You say that as if it were some kind of prison sentence."

"In a way it is."

"How's that?"

"I don't know. Marriage has always stood for boredom, frustration, and diapers."

"You make it sould pretty grim."

"Well, that's the way I think of it. My parents had such a lousy marriage. My mom never had any fun."

"Your marriage doesn't have to be that way."

"I know. But I'm afraid that's what's going to happen."

"I see."

"Besides, Hal and I are having a lot of fun living together."

"It sound as if you would like to go on living together indefinitely."

"That's right! That would be great."

"Well, why don't you?"

"Why don't we what?"

"Why don't you go on living together?"

"We have to get married sometime. We might as well get it over with."

"I don't see why you have to get married."

"Sooner or later, we're going to have to make up our minds."

"So why don't you make up your minds to live together permanently?"

"Oh, we could never do that."

"Why not?"

"Well, for one thing, our parents would never stand for it."

"Are your parents going to make this decision for you?"

"No, but—"

"I know. You're going to give me all the reasons why you don't want to hurt your parents. I understand that. I just think this question is too important to let anyone else decide."

"Maybe you're right."

Charlotte and I talked on several occasions after that. She had never considered the possibility of a permanent relationship outside of marriage. I believe our talks opened up that possibility. When I last saw her she was weighing her options a little more carefully. My guess is that she and Hal will finally get married. The difference is that their marriage will be more of a choice than it would have been the day she first came to see me.

The Security Blanket

The vast majority of couples who first lived together say that marriage changed their relationship. Even many couples who appear externally unchanged by marriage say their attitudes were affected once they had exchanged vows. Often they are not even sure how their relationship changed. As one young man said to me, "I could never explain the difference marriage made. I only know I have an entirely new attitude toward Karen now."

Other couples are able to talk about the changes marriage brought into their relationship. A great number of those who do attempt to describe their new attitudes talk about the greater security marriage brings. One young woman said, "Now I know there is a special bond linking us. I feel a lot more at ease just knowing that." Such feelings are understandable. The societal, religious, and legal sanctions bestowed on marriage would be expected to give couples a greater sense of security.

There is little doubt that many couples benefit from this extra sense of security. Some need to relax from the preoccupations of courtship and turn to other things. If they were to maintain the unmarried relationship too long, they would begin to feel stress from their temporary relationship. Those who tend to be fearful of separation might do well to make the formal commitments marriage demands.

For others, marriage can be destructive to the relationship. There are those, for example, who are too quick to take their relationship for granted. Even when they are living together, such couples are not very sensitive to one another. They too readily make assumptions, overlook moods, and impose expectations. The security of marriage could easily lead them to become even less sensitive. These couples might do well to consider living in an unmarried relationship permanently.

Even after they had lived together for two years, Maury and Jeannette lacked sensitivity to one another. Maury himself wondered why they had ever married. "I don't know what ever prompted us to get married," he admitted to me one day.

"What do you mean?"

"Well, we had such a good thing going while we were living together. Now we have grown apart."

"You mean marriage drew you apart?"

"I know that sounds strange, but that's just what happened."

"How did it happen?"

"I'm not sure."

"Well, how do you know that your relationship has suffered?"

"That's an easier question to answer. Almost as soon as we got married, I started paying more attention to other women."

"I'm beginning to understand."

"I know that sounds awful and I don't like to admit it, but that's what happened."

"Other women looked more interesting."

"Not only that, but I started to take Jeannette for granted. I would forget to tell her I was going to be late. I forgot an anniversary. A lot of little things like that, but behind them an important attitude was developing."

"You were becoming insensitive to Jeannette."

"I honestly think we had a better relationship when we were living together."

"Do you have any idea why?"

"I think so. I think I need to know that Jeannette might not be there in the morning. While we were living together, I was afraid she would leave me for another guy."

"Marriage doesn't change that. She could still leave you."

"I suppose she could, but somehow it doesn't seem that way."

"It sounds as if marriage took away your need to work on your relationship, and you began to think of Jeannette as a possession."

"That's right. Now I know it would take a divorce and a lot of legal hassle to pull us apart. So I can relax."

"But you're not relaxed."

"You're right. This is awful. I want to pay more attention to Jeannette, but I can't seem to bring myself to do it."

Jeannette felt the same way. She had come to take Maury for granted and also thought their relationship was suffering. They resolved their crisis in a unique way. After about a year of trying to improve their relationship without success, they decided to get a divorce. The resulting separation did not immediately improve their relationship. There was more to their difficulty than was obvious. But those differences gradually resolved themselves. Now they are living to-

gether again in the unmarried relationship. They
may or may not continue to resist marriage. But
the last time I talked to them, both Maury and
Jeannette were convinced they will never risk
marrying again.

Give Me Room

Some people choose to live together
permanently in order to retain their freedom.
Such couples fear they will find happiness in
marriage only after they sacrifice their independence. They see others depending on their marriage vows to hold their union together, rather
than working on the quality of their relationship. Couples living together do not want to hold
their relationship together by using such restrictions. At that point, they would surely have
given up a great deal of freedom.

Naturally, there are also those who find more
freedom in marriage. Some couples choose marriage in order to free themselves from working
so hard on their relationship. The insecurity of
living together can force some to put far too
much time and energy into their relationship.

One young woman put it very clearly.
"Before we were married," she said, "I didn't
have time for anyone else. I was preoccupied
with my relationship to Ned. Now that we are
married, I can begin to see how many people I
have shut out of my life."

Again we are faced with the complexities of
the individual. Each form of relationship will affect persons differently. To some, marriage will
give more freedom; to others, it will take freedom away. As our society allows couples more

freedom to choose different forms of relating, it will also make possible more than one kind of permanent relationship.

When I first met Gary, I was impressed immediately by the fact that he had been living with Alice for fourteen years. "That has to be some kind of record," I told him.

"I seriously doubt it. But it has been a long time."

"Did you ever think of getting married?"

"Oh, we talk about it regularly, but so far it hasn't suited us."

"Why not?"

"Lots of reasons. Every time we talk about marriage, we seem to decide against it for different reasons."

"No one reason stands out."

"Not really. I guess you would have to say we have never seen any evidence that marriage would add anything to our relationship. And we are convinced it could take away a great deal."

"I'm curious. What could marriage take away from your relationship?"

"Freedom."

"In what way?"

"I'm not really sure. It's just that we have seen so many of our friends get married. In some cases it worked out fine. Other times, it appeared that marriage was restricting them."

"Restricting them?"

"Yeah! They would feel they couldn't do this or that, or they had to do the other thing 'because they were married.' The restrictions were never real, but they might as well have been."

"But you and Alice are pretty mature. Don't

you think you could avoid those self-imposed restrictions?"

"I'm not sure. I've heard a lot of couples tell me they would never fall into that trap. Yet, soon after marriage, they were playing the same game."

"So you're convinced marriage would hurt your relationship."

"Oh, no. I'm not saying that at all. It's just that I'm afraid marriage might hurt it. I would rather not take that chance."

If every couple reflected as carefully as Gary and Alice did about their decision, we would probably have many more couples living together. The pressure toward marriage is so great that many couples unsuited for that relationship choose it without seriously considering the possible ramifications. Such couples would be far better off living together until the advantages of marriage became more obvious.

For the Kids

Many unmarried couples have said to me, in one way or another, "Of course if we want kids, we will have to get married." This attitude is widespread among those who are living together, but the lack of thought that surrounds it is disconcerting. Few of those I have questioned about this attitude give me any indication they have reflected much on it. It rather seems to be a premise that is accepted at face value.

This attitude is frightening because of the precedent it has in marriage. So many couples in unhappy marriages have said over the years, "We must stay together for the children." It does

not seem to matter how destructive such relationships are for the children. Nothing seems
to convince parents that their rule, "Children
need marriage," might be flawed.

Ironically, some of the staunchest defenders
of the marriage-before-children rule were victims of loveless marriages. They can tell you
about their tortured childhoods. I even heard one
young women say, "I wished one of them would
die. And I really didn't care which one. All I
wanted was some relief from the constant fighting and bickering." That sort of childhood experience clearly explains a person's need to
avoid marriage. What it fails to explain is the
same person's belief that children need to grow
up in the atmosphere of marriage.

If all relationships in marriage achieved the
ideal we have set for that institution, there might
be a case for marriage-before-children as an in-
flexible rule. But reality does not often achieve
the ideal. In those marriages that do reflect the
ideal, children will find happiness. Partners who
care deeply about one another and intend to remain unmarried need not be denied children,
however.

"But suppose we separate. Children, especially young children, need both parents,"
Mimi told me.

"Let's assume you're right. There is no way
to prove children need both parents in order to
grow up well-adjusted, but let's assume they do
for a few minutes."

"Good."

"Now, what makes you think that marriage
is going to keep you and Phil together?"

"You're turning my argument around on me, aren't you?"

"You're darn right I am. Just a few months ago you were laughing at the people who defend marriage."

"That was different. That was just between Phil and me. Now we're talking about a third person—a child."

"And you're going to guarantee your relationship will last by getting married?"

"Not forever. Just for the first few years of our child's life."

"Just what makes you think marriage will preserve your relationship even one day?"

"Well, if we both promise—"

"Promise to stay together no matter what?"

"Why not?"

"Didn't you tell me your own parents did just that? And that your childhood was pretty ugly until your father left home?"

"But it's not that way with Phil and me. We have a good relationship."

"I know you do. I think you and Phil would make great parents. The only thing that scares me is your attempt to keep it good by getting married."

"Why are you so set against Phil and me getting married?"

"Wait a minute! I'm not against your getting married. If I gave that impression, I'm sorry."

"Now I am confused."

"If you and Phil decide the attraction between you is so strong that you want to stay together indefinitely, that's great. Get married. I just don't want to see you forced into making promises that are prompted by forces outside of you."

"You mean you would like to see marriage reserved for those who already feel their love is going to hold them together indefinitely."

"Exactly."

"What about children?"

"You might want to wait until you are sure the bond between you and Phil is strong enough to last through the first few years of your child's life."

"How can I be sure?"

"You can't. But then there is no certitude that a child needs two parents to be happy. I know a lot of happy, well adjusted kids who have only one parent."

"That's true, isn't it."

This discussion has not touched on the social stigma attached to illegitimacy. I do not want to ignore that attitude. It is one of the most degrading labels that can be attached to anyone. Any child born out of wedlock now will surely suffer from such attitudes. Even the most rapid social change will not entirely erase the deep prejudice our society still holds against the "illegitimate."

I am not saying anyone should ignore the serious problems implicit in beginning a family before marriage. Rather, I am saying that most couples think of nothing else. They have heard the rules like marriage-before-children for so long that they are blinded to other possibilities. And there are other possibilities. There is a possibility that a given couple, along with their children, will be happier if they never get married. I would like everyone to consider that possibility.

Something New

The arguments against living together are breaking down. More and more couples are trying that kind of relationship as a way of getting to know each other. Living together as a permanent life-style is also emerging. The arguments against it are being considered more carefully than ever before. There is every indication that it will eventually be an option for every couple.

As this new form of relating becomes more popular, I have only one hope: I hope that couples will not blindly enter the unmarried relationship the way so many have blindly entered marriage. Already couples are feeling pressure from their peers to live together before they marry. This is unfortunate. Pressures only make prudent decisions more difficult. Couples must consider their attitudes carefully and make sure their choice is based on those personal attitudes. Those who are swayed by forces outside of themselves are risking their relationship.

The hopeful thing about this new form of relating is the alternative it gives people. It was not available just a few years ago. Those who could have benefitted from getting to know one another on a day-to-day basis before marriage were not free to live together openly. Outside of limited times together, all but the most courageous were not going to see the more natural side of their relationship until they were married.

The points presented in the last page or so sum up the attitudes I brought to this book. I have no desire to defend the unmarried relationship. It needs no defense. Neither does it need any promotion. Only time stands between the present situation and acceptance of living together as a viable option, and I hoped to look at this new social relationship with the same critical eye that has been brought to bear on marriage. Living together is no more a panacea than marriage has proved to be. Certainly many flaws mar both forms of relating. As living together becomes more acceptable, however, we can be proud of ourselves as a society. We have expanded our horizons just a little bit and given ourselves another option.

A recent conversation with a friend says a great deal about the future of the unmarried relationship. Pete told me one day of his mother's violent opposition from the day he moved in with Pam.

"What was her objection?" I inquired. "Didn't she like Pam?"

"Oh, yes. She was crazy about Pam."

"What was the problem, then?"

"Mom's religion."

"Oh, she had some moral problems about the way you were living."

"That's putting it mildly. My mom was a religious fanatic."

"*Was* a religious fanatic?"

"That's the amazing thing. When Pam and I first started living together, my mother nearly went crazy. To hear her tell it, we were both going straight to hell."

"How about now?"

"Well, over the past two years she has gotten used to the idea."

"In what way?"

"In a lot of ways. She quit condemning us to hell. She started talking to both of us as if we were two people who loved each other."

"Did she accept your desire to remain unmarried?"

"That took a lot longer. In fact, it wasn't until last week that I knew her attitude had really changed."

"What convinced you of that?"

"Mom told me she wished she had lived with my father for a while before they got married."

"Really?"

"Really! Of course she was quick to tell me that she never would have thought of marrying anyone else. But she said she thought it might have been a good idea to get to know my dad a little better before she took the final step."

"From religious fanatic to that kind of understanding in only two years."

"Those were two long and hard years."

"I know. But still—"

"Yeah, it is pretty amazing isn't it?"

Like so many of the examples I have used, this is an extreme case. But it points up the possibilities. If just one person can open up a thoroughly rigid position, then the attitudes of society will certainly change. Parents of couples who live together are generally, with great misgivings, of course, discovering the wisdom that living together can represent. In that way, two generations are beginning to accept the unmarried relationship.

No one can ask for more.

Index